Not Fade Away

Not Fade Away

A Memoir of Senses Lost and Found

Rebecca Alexander

with
Sascha Alper

GOTHAM BOOKS

GOTHAM BOOKS
Published by the Penguin Group
Penguin Group (USA) LLC
375 Hudson Street
New York, New York 10014

USA | Canada | UK | Ireland | Australia | New Zealand | India | South Africa | China
penguin.com
A Penguin Random House Company

Library of Congress Cataloging-in-Publication Data

Alexander, Rebecca (Psychotherapist)
  Not fade away : a memoir of senses lost and found / by Rebecca Alexander with Sascha Alper.
      pages cm
  ISBN 978-1-59240-831-3 (hardback)
  1. Alexander, Rebecca (Psychotherapist)—Health.   2. Retinitis pigmentosa—Patients—United States—Biography.   3. Usher's syndrome—Patients—United States—Biography.
4. People with disabilities—United States—Biography.   I. Alper, Sascha.   II. Title.
  RE661.R45A44 2014
  617.7'35092—dc23
  [B]
                                        2014008690

Printed in the United States of America
10 9 8 7 6 5 4 3 2 1

Set in Adobe Garamond Pro
Designed by Spring Hoteling

This book is dedicated to the two most influential women in my life: my mother, Terry Pink Alexander, and my stepmother, Pauline Fox.

*Kindness is the language which the deaf
can hear and the blind can see.*

—Mark Twain

*Although the world is full of suffering,
it is full also of the overcoming of it.*

—Helen Keller

Not Fade Away

1

Even though the doctor's office was warm, I was freezing. A nineteen-year-old California girl in the midst of my first winter at the University of Michigan, I couldn't shake the cold that seemed to seep into everything. Though my hair and many layers of clothes had long since dried from my wintry trek through piles of mounting snow to the school's medical campus, I could still feel the chill in the constant ache down my leg and into my foot that never quite went away, making my limp even more pronounced.

The office was spare and bright, and as I sat there, aimlessly looking around, legs tucked under me as I absently rubbed my stiff ankle, I thought about how many rooms I'd been in just like this one. Days of tests and waiting, and more tests, and more waiting. This time I was here for the ringing in my ears, a relentless noise that had followed me for weeks, perpetually making me feel as though I had just left the loudest rock concert imaginable. Sometimes it completely drowned out other noises; at other times it whined incessantly in the background, keeping me awake at night, making me feel as though I was losing my mind. I knew what it was called—tinnitus, from the Latin word meaning "to ring"—but that didn't come close to describing what I was experiencing. It felt as though it was coming from inside *and* outside of my head, reverberating against my eardrums, something so obviously real that it seemed impossible that nobody else could hear it. When someone spoke to me, no matter how quiet it was around us, I felt like I needed them to raise their voice above it, the way they would if a fire engine were screaming by, or, better yet, speak directly into my ear. *Please just let this go away,* I kept thinking. What I didn't know at the time was that the ringing would never go away, that it would become my constant companion, and that in time I would learn to tune it out almost completely, a noise so familiar that I would sometimes have to strain to hear it at all.

The door opened, and a doctor who appeared to be in his midforties walked in, followed by a few awkward-looking residents who quickly jockeyed for place around him, all trying to get a good look at the patient. The doctor, brisk and forthright, asked if they could stay while he went over my diagnosis with me. I nodded, smiling at them, feeling bad because I could tell that things were not good, and that they were going to have to listen to the doctor give a diagnosis that none of us wanted to hear. But they averted their eyes from my gaze, looking busily down at their clipboards, not yet having mastered the specialist's casual smile: persistent, even in the face of very bad news.

· · · ·

Though we weren't aware that anything was wrong until I was twelve, it was there all along, lying in wait, showing itself in ways too subtle at first to notice. Ours was always the fun, boisterous house, the one all of the neighborhood kids wanted to hang out at, full of laughter, music, and roughhousing. My brothers and I were athletic: heedlessly racing, chasing and slugging it out when we fought. When our friends came over we would take countless screaming, bumpy rides in our sleeping bags down our long stairway and run wildly through the house. All of which probably made it harder to notice my clumsiness—though I was always the one tripping over things, banging into them, getting hurt. Being the only girl of the three of us, I shook it off, determined to be as tough as my brothers were. Even though Daniel and I were twins, while Peter was three years older, I always felt like the youngest, trailing after Daniel—brilliant, athletic, beautiful Dan, already the superstar of everything—determined to try to keep up.

In ballet, too, I was the clumsy one, awkward and off-kilter. In my pink tights and tight bun that I brushed incessantly to keep smooth, I was so eager to be graceful. But no matter how hard I tried I could never maintain my balance while holding my positions or float across the floor like the other girls. My stern, ramrod-straight instructor scolded "Rebecca" so often that I began to sneak out of class, hiding in the dressing room and eating my snack of Goldfish crackers in an attempt to avoid further humiliation.

There were other signs, too, like the way I would turn my head sideways to watch TV, cocking my left ear toward it while looking out of the corners of my eyes, or the way I seemed to tune out sometimes, especially when I sat in the back of the classroom, leading my teachers to refer to me as a "dreamer," which even then I knew was code for "not paying attention." But none of this was out of the ordinary enough to catch anyone's attention in our busy, noisy household.

Really, though, it goes back so much further than my childhood, long before Daniel and I floated safely together inside my mother, a yin-yang of boy and girl curled against one another, when no one could have imagined the terrible and wonderful things growing inside of each of us. Back to Eastern Europe, most likely Kiev, where both of my parents had ancestors. Their numbers shrunk from countless pogroms, cousins would marry, and carry with them a single mutated gene that ended up here, inside of me, invisible, until at twelve I started having trouble seeing the blackboard.

. . . .

Although our house was a loud one, with rarely a silent moment, as a younger child I remember it as mostly joyful noise—laughing, talking, and lots of singing. We each tried our best to be more clever than the next, knowing that it pleased our parents, rapid-fire jokes and witty retorts tossed back and forth. My mother had at one time sung professionally, and we would often crowd around her at the piano, belting out show tunes as dramatically as if we were on Broadway, until she would stand up and lead us singing and dancing up the stairs to do our homework. Quiet felt so strange to me that I used to feel uncomfortable when I was alone, turning on the television or music for noise, much happier and better able to relax with plenty going on around me—so different from now, when silence often feels like my salvation.

That all changed when I was ten, a couple of years before we started to notice my vision problems, when a new noise started creeping around our house. At first it was barely noticeable, angry whispers through gritted teeth. Eventually my parents' fights grew louder, screaming matches where my brothers and I would race in, pleading for them to stop or trying to entertain them, anything to make it go away. By the time they started to notice something was wrong with me, they were already separated, caught in that hazy "trying to work it out" phase, which we could all tell wasn't working.

My dad had taken me to the optometrist after I told him that I was having trouble seeing the blackboard at school, assuming that I needed glasses. The doctor had frowned through much of the exam—a look I've gotten to know well over the years—and at the end of the appointment told my dad that he had seen something in the back of my eye that needed to be examined more thoroughly, but he didn't have the equipment or the expertise to properly evaluate it. So we were referred to an ophthalmologist, and then another one, and another. We went to see specialists at the University of California–San Francisco and Stanford, and eye charts were replaced with increasingly complex equipment and tests, one of which required me to have hard lenses with wires coming out of them attached to my eyeballs, while another had me staring at bright flashing lights as long as I could without blinking. I kept thinking, *All this just to get glasses?*

Each time, I waited for the doctor to come out with a smile, to nod and tell us that he'd figured it out, that things were just fine, they'd fix me right up. In one test I was given several times, I would sometimes press the button to signify that I'd seen the little flashing light even when I hadn't, wanting to make everyone proud. I wanted to ace these eye tests, to have everyone tell me I had done a great job, to get to leave and pick out a cute pair of glasses, go home and stop thinking about my eyes and my parents' fights and their worried glances at me. I wanted to worry about twelve-year-old things, hanging out with my friends and spending hours on the phone with them, talking about boys, what we would wear to the upcoming middle school dance, and whether or not one boy or another liked us as "more than just a friend."

Eventually, the diagnosis came. The doctors told my parents that they thought I had something called "retinitis pigmentosa," an incurable, inherited disorder that meant the cells in my retina were slowly dying. They explained that I would most likely be blind by the time I was an adult, and my parents had to decide how to break this news to me. How do you tell your child this? What words can you possibly find to explain this to a young girl? I can't imagine their heartbreak, knowing that someday their daughter would no longer be able to see them, or her brothers, or the world around her.

From the start my mother was convinced that I should have all the information, that it was my body and that the more I knew, the more I could prepare and find ways to help myself face, emotionally and physically, what lay ahead. If I knew, she argued, I would understand why some things were hard for me, that it wasn't my fault that I couldn't see a tennis ball coming, or had so much trouble in dance, or couldn't see my way to the bathroom at night without banging into things. She knew this was a challenge I had no choice but to rise to and fully believed that even at my age I should be allowed the responsibility of understanding.

My father vehemently disagreed. I was, in his eyes, still his little girl. He was terrified that I would hear what he referred to in a whispered hiss as "the b-word"—*blind*. He thought that I should be given the information slowly, over time, so that I could digest it. He had all of the literature from the hospital and the Foundation Fighting Blindness sent to his office, so that I wouldn't see any of it. At first all that I understood was that my vision was getting worse, and that it would become even harder to see at night. The rest would come slowly, the progression of the decline in my vision and hearing subtle enough from day to day that the realization, when I was young, never hit me full force. I'm not sure, though, that even if my parents had told me everything from the start, I would have been able to comprehend it. How could a twelve-year-old possibly imagine going blind?

. . . .

At nineteen, back in the warm office in Michigan, the doctor sat down across from me, the interns flanking him shifting uncomfortably as he delivered my diagnosis. He spoke kindly but directly—no sugarcoating here: I was going blind and deaf.

He told me it was a genetic disorder, one as of yet undocumented in the way it presented in me, but he had his suspicions all the same. Usher syndrome was his hunch, the symptoms that characterized it being simultaneous hearing and vision loss, though thus far he had only seen it affect people much younger, who were either born deaf and blind or had it present in early childhood. At that point none of these seemingly trivial details mattered to me, it was only the first sentence that I heard. The words pounded like a drumbeat in my head—*blinddeaf blinddeaf blinddeaf*—drowning out even the tinnitus. Still I tried to smile, nod at the right times, always be the good patient.

Looking back, it shouldn't have come as a shock. It wasn't the first time I'd heard "blind" or "deaf." I knew that my vision was deteriorating more quickly, and my hearing was getting worse, too. Maybe I hadn't been ready to hear it before, but this was the first time that a doctor had laid it all out for me, making sure that I understood. And I did. For the first time I actually really heard it. Me. Blind. Deaf. No cure, no stopping it.

I tried to think, to ask him questions about what I should expect and how fast it would progress. But they were all met with a gentle shake of his head and a simple, "I'm sorry, we just don't know." When we were done, I smiled, thanked him, and stood up. I stayed composed, said good-bye to the other doctors, and walked out, trying not to let my limp show, knowing that they must have pitied me enough already. I left the hospital, surrounded by great walls of shoveled snow, but this time I hardly noticed the cold.

By the time I got back to my dorm, I knew what I would do with what I had just learned: nothing. I didn't call my parents immediately or go find Daniel, somewhere on campus, no doubt surrounded by a throng of friends and admirers. I went back to my room and took off my hat, shaking my long dark hair around my ears, making sure that it completely covered my hearing aids. I knew that I would still take them out and slip them under my mattress when I brought a guy back to my room, that I would do everything I could to compensate for my diminishing vision without talking about it. Sometimes it felt like a character defect, the same way it had when I was twelve. If I had just done better on all those tests, maybe my parents wouldn't be divorced, maybe I wouldn't have had the accident, maybe somehow I could just rewind it all and not be here, knowing what I was going to lose. Which, at the time, felt like everything.

2

Ashkenazi genetic disorders are common. Tay-Sachs, a devastating, progressive disease of the nervous system, is probably the most well-known, but there are many, and it's estimated that one in four people of Eastern European Jewish ancestry is a carrier for one of them. These disorders come from a recessive genetic mutation, and, since genes come in pairs, if only one is mutated, you don't get the syndrome, but you'll carry the gene with you. There are now simple blood tests for many of them, since, if both parents are carriers, there is a 25 percent chance that the child will inherit it. If only one parent is a carrier, it is harmless. Well, "harmless" being a relative term. Maybe "dormant" is a better word.

Usher syndrome is rare enough that most people have never heard of it. It was named for the British ophthalmologist Charles Usher, who in 1914 discovered a common defect among sixty-nine deaf-and-blind people that he'd studied.

Children who are born with Usher syndrome type I are profoundly or completely deaf at birth; suffer severe imbalance due to vertigo, as their inner ear doesn't function properly; and usually don't benefit from the use of hearing aids. By around ten they start to lose their sight and then generally go blind very quickly.

Type II is a little less severe. Children are usually born with some hearing loss but tend to have normal balance and generally keep at least some vision until their teens.

My Usher, type III, is the least severe, which makes me comparatively lucky, if you look at it that way. And why not look at it that way? Any vision or hearing loss I had at birth was undetectable. The onset is slow, and subtle at first, and you are not generally blind and deaf until you are an adult.

There was a time before I was living with the constant reminder that I was going blind and deaf, and for that I feel incredibly grateful. My mother felt guilty about not noticing my symptoms sooner, but since there was nothing that she could have done, it seems better to have had those blissful years of ignorance. It wasn't even possible, until a long time later, for our family to be tested for the gene, because at that point, nobody could even prove its existence. There were years where my parents didn't worry, didn't fear for their daughter, and didn't feel the heartbreak of knowing the things that I would lose, or might never have.

For me, those were years of not being treated differently or feeling isolated, of having a chance to gain some sense of myself before this became part of who I was and who I would become. I feel so lucky that my disabilities didn't define me as a child and for what my eyes and ears have had a chance to experience. I have been able to see so much beauty, to read, to look into people's eyes, and to hear music and laughter and the voices of everyone I love. I have created memories that will stay with me long after my eyes and ears have lost their ability to capture new ones.

3

A normally sighted person can see one hundred eighty degrees without turning her head. Today, I can see less than ten. The scientific explanation for retinitis pigmentosa, or RP, is that the retina, made up of photoreceptor cells, those rods and cones we learn about in science class, die. But the better understanding of what it's really like is described by its common nickname, "donut vision." I have a donut-shaped ring of blindness floating in my field of vision, and the donut gets bigger and the hole gets smaller every day. I have a sliver of vision left on the outside of the donut, at the outermost edge of my peripheral vision, and I can see straight ahead through the hole. But everything else, all of the donut, is gone. I'm left with about a square foot of vision directly in front of me, and every day, a little bit more of the world is taken from me. It sometimes feels like the end of one of those old Warner Bros. cartoons on TV, where Bugs Bunny sits in the center of the screen waving good-bye as the picture becomes an increasingly smaller hole, until it's finally gone, leaving only blackness. *That's all, folks.*

For a while, when my eyesight first started to deteriorate, if I was somewhere familiar my memory would fill in what I couldn't see. When I was younger I would move my eyes rapidly from side to side, scanning to be able to piece together a complete picture. I still do this, but as my vision loss has progressed, the donut hole becoming increasingly smaller, I can no longer overcome the blind spots. People now appear in front of me as if out of nowhere. I'm unable to see them approach me from my periphery, and then suddenly there they are, in the tiny center hole of my vision. It's like a startling and unpleasant magic trick, one that I never get used to.

Often, my brain creates made-up images in an attempt to compensate for the vision I no longer have—for a long time, I kept a frying pan by my desk at home because when I was at the computer, my brain kept projecting a peripheral image of a man walking through my apartment, or sometimes standing right at my shoulder. With a huge gasp, I would jump out of my chair, and then, like in a horror movie, he would be gone.

When I'm sitting across from someone in anything but bright light, I can no longer see their full face. I can't see their expressions: what's going on between their eyes and their mouth, how their cheeks are moving or the arch of their eyebrows, the subtle shake or nod of their head. I can see pieces, but never the whole picture. If I'm introduced to someone in a dark, noisy room—like a dimly lit bar or restaurant—not only do I usually miss the name of the person I'm being introduced to, I generally have no idea where they're standing, and I don't know where I should be sticking my hand out to greet them, so I just give it my best shot. I usually get it wrong, and sometimes I don't even know if I'm meeting a man or a woman. Once, in a crowded club full of pounding music, a friend introduced me to a guy she knew and left me alone with him while she went to get us drinks. I leaned in toward him a few times to comment on the music and the crowd, despite the fact that I could barely see or hear him. I'm not sure when he wandered away, or if he said good-bye, but I kept right on talking, and then reached out to touch his arm at one point and realized that, for at least a few minutes, I had been talking to a large column next to our table. Before I'd even had a drink. Luckily, I couldn't see enough to note the reactions of the people around me. Though really, I'm so used to not seeing or mishearing people that I'm almost beyond embarrassment. When something like that happens, I have to laugh. What's the alternative? The doctors who diagnosed me thought I'd be blind by the time I was thirty. I'm thirty-four now, and every day that I wake up and can still see is a gift.

Every day, the cartoon hole closes in on me, and I push back against it with all my might.

4

The first lie I can remember telling was when I was seven years old. It was late one afternoon, and I heard the faint, magical tune of the ice cream truck. Whenever we started to hear it—and sometimes, unimaginable now, I would even be the first to—my brothers and I would drop everything and perk up our ears, like dogs intently focused on a sound in the distance. We'd stay frozen until the tune became loud enough for us to realize that this was our chance, and then we'd chase each other up the long flight of stairs from the backyard into the house directly to our piggy banks, grab our precious coins, and jump down the stairs two or three at a time, flying out the front door just as the ice cream man was slowly cruising by our house.

On one such afternoon I raced in and opened my piggy bank, and found nothing but a few dark brown, tarnished pennies lying there. I thought quickly, and right after I heard Danny race back down the stairs, I ran into his room to "borrow" some of his change to buy my ice cream. I didn't know if he'd find out, but I knew that no matter what I would deny it at all cost. Of course he noticed, and my mother asked me later that evening if I had taken his money. Though the Good Humor strawberry shortcake ice cream bar I had eaten hours before weighed heavily in my stomach, I was sure that if I just kept denying it, it would mean that I wasn't really the one who had done it, so that's exactly what I did. I denied it, despite there being no way that anybody else could have taken it, despite the fact that I'm sure they all knew it was me. It didn't matter, because I knew I couldn't bear the disappointment in my mother's voice if I admitted it. I already felt like a huge disappointment to my mom for not being the little girl she wanted me to be.

If you asked my mother, she would say that I was the most beautiful, precious, perfect little girl. And she would mean it. She would say that she couldn't be more proud of me, that I am extraordinary and wonderful, that I have done anything a fully sighted and hearing person could do and more. And she would believe it with all of her heart. But that was never what I thought. I knew I could never be anything like my mother, who could do anything and everything, and do it all with grace and charm. She was so beautiful, and feminine, and competent, and there was a part of me that thought I wasn't what she wanted in a daughter. I was sure, though, that I knew exactly what she did want: for me to be just like my best friend, Melissa Neuwelt.

Melissa was perfect. She was little and tidy, with small, slender hands, and she played the piano beautifully. She had lovely features, a tiny nose, and absolutely no freckles. She was very smart, well behaved, and polite to a fault. She was any parent's dream child. Of course, my mother adored her. And so, of course, I bullied her when she would come over, and when she threatened to tell on me to my mom, I locked her in my bedroom, barring the door. The minute I let her out she ran directly to my mother's room and leapt straight into her arms. As I watched my mother comfort her, I felt terrible and guilty. But I also hated her, for being able to be so good and honest all the time.

I, on the other hand, saw myself as clumsy and lumbering, dreamy and messy, too sporty. I tried to be what I thought my mother wanted me to be, but I knew deep down that I wasn't. For as long as I could remember I had felt like I had to be someone different from who I was. And I was sure, even at seven, that I just wasn't good enough. I was sneaky, and I lied, and, even if other people didn't realize it, I knew that I wasn't a good girl.

Where do we get these ideas about ourselves? In my practice as a psychotherapist, I see people every day who are still trapped in the patterns that they learned when they were young, the things that they believed about themselves as children remaining with them every day. I knew that there were differences between my mother and me, and because I so desperately wanted to be like her, I was sure that every difference was a fault.

When I turned eight, my mom threw me a doll party. This must have been her idea, because I was not one of those girls who carried her dollies everywhere. But once she said it, all I wanted was a Cabbage Patch doll for my birthday, and they were sold out everywhere. That was at the height of the insane Cabbage Patch craze, and they were impossible to find. Of course, Melissa had one of the preemies, the most sought-after Cabbage Patch dolls of all. She brought it to my party, carrying it like a real baby and looking darling in her pretty dress sprinkled with tiny little flowers. There were doll centerpieces, doilies, and Cabbage Patch plates and napkins, all as girly as could be. This was not the party I would have chosen, but I did my best to play the part. My mom came to the table and taught us lullabies to sing to our dolls. The irony was that while the other girls had their little dolls, I had

Montgomery Moose, Daniel's favorite stuffed animal from the Get Along Gang. My mother sang in her beautiful voice, and all the little girls loved it, except me. There is a home video of this event, which shows Melissa holding her baby in just the right way, gently stroking her perfectly swaddled little preemie as she sings sweetly to her. I am sitting at the head of the table in a big chair that Danny is sharing with me, looking off somewhere, not paying much attention to the goings-on, Montgomery Moose resting listlessly in my arms. Danny had a Western-themed party. I had more fun at his.

I wasn't a particularly smart child, but what I lacked in intelligence, I made up for with my imagination. I had such an active world in my head. I know now that when my teachers said that I was a daydreamer or had my head in the clouds, some of that must have been because I couldn't see or hear them as well as I should have. Still, they weren't wrong. I liked my imaginary world much more, because I could be anyone that I wanted to be. I could take all of the things that I thought were wrong with me and replace them with beautiful ones. I would do this when falling asleep at night, because I was terribly afraid of the dark and suffered from nightmares. For years I slept in Daniel's room, because I had seen *Friday the 13th* at a friend's house when I was far too young and refused to sleep alone. Then I taught myself a trick where I would replay the same happy story again and again in my head until I fell asleep. When I was young I would fantasize about dancing as Clara from *The Nutcracker,* and as I got older I would imagine that a boy whom I liked was about to kiss me, and as soon as he leaned in toward me, I'd replay the scene over and over, until I was asleep.

My imagination was not exclusive to my dreams. I spent years of my childhood telling lies that I'd created so vividly in my head that even I believed them. They were never malicious, and as a young child I mostly told them to avoid getting in trouble, but they came easily.

As I got older, my lies became more elaborate, and, like dominoes set up one after another, each one led to more lies as I tried to cover them up. They were absurd, too, and totally unnecessary, but I always felt an overwhelming need to make myself seem better than I was.

In seventh grade I remember talking on the phone to a guy I liked and was trying to impress by telling him that I was related to Cindy Crawford, thinking somehow that this might make me worthy of him. It sounds absurd now and I can laugh about it, but at the time, I was desperate for approval. I just thought I needed something to make me seem better, cooler, different.

I told another guy whom I was trying to impress that I was going to be doing a photo shoot for *Seventeen* magazine and that I needed to choose a guy to be in it with me. I wrote down a list of questions to ask him about what he'd want to wear and how he'd want to be positioned in the shoot. I sat in the kitchen on the phone, twirling the phone cord as I actually wrote down his answers to these questions, nearly believing the ridiculous things that I was saying. I remember at one point a group of these boys called me and made fun of me for the lies I'd told. And just as I had when I was a little girl, I denied, denied, denied.

Perhaps this is part of why, when we found out that there was something wrong with my eyes, it didn't surprise me as much as it might have. Instead, it confirmed what I already knew about myself. I wasn't like other people. I had been right: I was deeply flawed, and I was never going to be perfect.

All of the lying was useful in one sense: It prepared me for the much bigger lies that were to come. I was well practiced by the time I was hiding my hearing aids, hiding my vision problems, and still doing everything I could to try to be just like everyone else.

Then I started to steal. My friend Jamie and I took lipstick from the drugstore one day, and when we found a cigarette on the ground while walking home that afternoon, we hid under the deck in my backyard, smoking in our bright stolen lipstick. When I was a teenager I started stealing more, from stores like J.Crew and Victoria's Secret. It was a release, a high, and I felt exhilarated every time I got away with it. There was a part of me that felt like the world owed me something. That was how I justified it as I got older. I was just evening the scales.

Of course, the world doesn't owe me anything. It doesn't owe any of us anything. It was me who owed the world, and myself, something: to be better than that. Though that's a lesson that I couldn't yet comprehend, one that I had to learn over and over again, until it finally stuck.

5

When I was a little girl I loved going to visit my mother's mother, Grandma Etta, in Santa Fe, New Mexico. I adore Grandma Etta, who is independent and free-spirited to this day, at ninety-two, still taking her morning swims in Lake Michigan and wearing beautiful Indian saris for festive occasions. When she would read to us she could do any accent and bring every character to life. My favorite was when Grandma would read me *Eloise.* She would capture her exuberant, naughty, childish voice perfectly, and I would sit, mesmerized, wishing she would go on forever.

I knew that we were getting close to Grandma's house when I began to bounce gently in my seat to the sound of the tiny rocks under our tires, which meant we were at the beginning of her driveway. An insignificant sound, but one that I loved and can still remember so clearly.

We would often go at Christmastime, and even though we were Jewish, on Christmas Eve Mom would put up little stockings for us, letting us enjoy a few of the perks that our friends did.

Then we would walk down the pebbled roads, where tea lights in white paper bags would be lined up on either side to celebrate the holiday, and down into the town, where the Native American women laid their jewelry out on blankets. They were in an array of vibrant colors: the gorgeous range of turquoise greens and blues, bracelets and barrettes intricately beaded in red and green and yellow. We watched the ceremonial dance performances and chants, the men in their beautiful headdresses moving to the beat of their powerful drums. I loved how different the colors were from those of Oakland and Berkeley, with their heavily paved roads and towering trees of eucalyptus, oak, and redwood. Here, the backdrop for the bright colors and stones was the subtler colors of the Southwest, earth tones of adobe, purple, and brown.

In the evening I would sit on the porch swing, with Grandma's dog, Tilly, a loyal German shepherd mix rescue dog, at my feet. I would absently stroke her with my toes as I watched the sun set in a brilliant wash of orange, red, and purple, and as the evening breeze picked up, the bells on Grandma's porch would start chiming. The bells and the sunset and Tilly's warm body beneath my feet filled me with so much joy.

The last time I remember seeing a sky full of stars was on one of those visits, when I was nine or ten years old. Once the sun had set, and the dark had brought in the chill, we would bundle up in our sweatshirts and sit outside of her little adobe house and look up at the universe filled with tiny pinpricks of light, the whole sky ours to see.

Today I live in Manhattan, where no one is able to see the stars anyway—but whenever I'm lucky enough to be in a place where they're visible, I'm sometimes able to see the very brightest ones. One, or sometimes two if I'm really lucky, though whomever I'm with assures me, when I ask, that the sky is full of them, twinkling diamonds in an inky-black sky. And this comforts, rather than distresses, me. To be able to see just one makes me so happy. I can still see a star, millions of miles away! The sky is still full of them, I have enough vision to see one, and my imagination can fill in the rest. Someday, I'll have to rely on my memory to conjure them, but I will have taken the time to look, and to be grateful.

For me, there are so many experiences that are limited or already gone, and so many more will be—some very soon—that it is impossible not to feel lucky now, while I still have them. I think that I am probably more grateful for that one star than I would be if I were fully sighted, looking at a whole sky shining with them.

6

My brothers and I all remember our family, and our child-hood, as an idyllic one. We were always close, physically affectionate, rolling on top of one another like puppies, fighting to see who could be the wittiest, be the funniest, get the most attention. My mother would come home after a full day of work and cook us a homemade meal, sing to us, and play the piano, and coordinated our busy schedules to and from soccer and bas-ketball practice and piano lessons. My father was loud, funny, and gregarious. He was tall and muscular, and when we were younger the three of us used to beg him to pick us all up at once and try to carry us around. There was nothing that frightened me more than when he raised his voice in anger at us, a rare event, but one that I dreaded. Our parents looked beautiful together, and I loved to look at pictures of the five of us hung around the house, my father next to my mother, dwarfing her, with his huge hand resting on her tiny shoulder, Peter, Danny, and I in front, grinning. I would run my fingers along the glass, stopping to rest the tip of one on each tiny face, and know with an absolute certainty that we were a perfect family.

The night my parents told us they were getting separated we had sat down to an early dinner, so used to my parents' strained conversation at this point that we barely noticed their silence as we chattered on about our day, talking over one another. They told us that after dinner we needed to go up to their room so that we could have a family meeting. We never had family meetings, and I remember nervously looking back and forth between my parents, who sat at either end of the kitchen table, not looking at us or at one another, trying to imagine what they possibly needed to speak to us about that couldn't be discussed right there at the dinner table. After we had cleared the table and helped clean the kitchen, Peter and Daniel raced and roughhoused their way up the stairs while I lagged behind, for once not feeling the need to keep up.

I had always loved my parents' bedroom. The lingering scent of my mom's perfume, my dad's shoe polish, and the crisp smell of his dry-cleaned work shirts greeted me each time I entered their room. Danny, Peter, and I would often lie on their bed in our PJs, making funny faces into the reflective brass globes that sat atop the bed frame, our grossly distorted features reflecting back at us from the round shapes of the balls, keeping us in hysterics until we were writhing in pain from our laughter. We loved to wake them up when we were little, racing in after Saturday morning cartoons to beg for my mom's French toast, or her matz-n-egg scramble, a family specialty, accompanied by my dad's fresh-squeezed orange juice. We would climb all over them, my mother's smell of sleep that I cherished and my father's faint smell of Irish Spring mingling into the warm comfort of exactly where we belonged.

That night, as we scrambled for our places on the bed, everyone wanting the middle, of course, my dad and mom slowly followed us in, closing the door behind them. My mom did most of the talking, and the only sentence I remember clearly is "Your dad and I have decided to separate." I'd only seen my mom cry a few times before—after a few of my parents' fiercer arguments—and I would feel so incredibly guilty, watching her cry and not knowing what to do to help her. This time, though, my dad was crying, too—inconsolably. I had never seen him cry, and I felt so helpless and terrified. My big, strong daddy falling apart was not something I could comprehend; it didn't fit in with the world I knew and the father I loved. It felt so utterly wrong that I began to feel nausea rising along with my sobs. And I knew he wasn't just crying for himself, but for the unbearable pain they were causing us.

What I didn't know then was that he was also crying out of guilt. Guilt that his own illness, his depression and mania—which my brothers and I knew nothing of at the time—had helped push this into motion. Behavior that I would someday recognize in my brother, another illness carried down, probably through generations as well. Right then, though, all that I saw was that the two people whom I loved most in the world were preparing to tear our world apart.

As my brothers and I pleaded and begged for them to reconsider or try to work it out, my father told us, between his sobs, that it was what he wanted, too, to try to keep our family together, to stay together and work on it. My mother was clearer. She told us that she could no longer tolerate her children running down the stairs to try to stop a fight between them. The last straw for her had been watching Daniel race into the dining room, shove himself between them, and plead, "Daddy! Daddy! Please don't hurt Mommy!" She couldn't bear the idea of us, her babies, feeling as though we had to protect her from my dad, and she did not want us to believe that our dad, who stood at least a foot taller than she did, could ever possibly hurt her.

Danny, Peter, and I asked desperate, heartbroken questions, believing, the way children do, that we could somehow change the outcome of the adult world. Despite watching my parents fight more and more, I really thought we had the perfect family. My mother and father explained that they were going to first try a "separation," though even then I could see by the look on my mother's face that this was my father's idea. We would stay in our house, and they would alternate staying with us. That sounded horrible to me, but still, I clung to it like a life raft. Surely, I thought, they would come to their senses.

This was the last time that we were all together in my parents' room.

. . . .

For a long time we existed in this strange limbo where my parents would take turns staying with us. My dad would stay in the in-law unit at a family friend's house when he was gone, and my mom rented a tiny basement room at the back of a neighborhood house, where I would sometimes want to stay, finding it too unbearable to be away from her for very long, and wanting to protect her and keep her company. I would lie huddled under a purple sleeping bag on the futon that I shared with her, in that lonely room, with nothing but a tiny bathroom and a mini fridge, and wonder how on earth it had come to this. How could she rather be here than with my dad, in our house? What could be so terrible that she would choose this over having our family together? I didn't blame her, though, because I, too, was some-times afraid of my dad's temper, though he was also the kindest, most generous man I knew. I just wanted things back the way that they had been.

Peter felt badly for my dad. He was the eldest and so strong in his conviction that we were the perfect family that he still says it to this day. Always the peacemaker, he just wanted my mom to give our dad another chance. At the time, Danny seemed to be the most unscathed of the three of us, walking the line as he con-tinued to get excellent grades in school and kick ass in every sport he played.

At the time, and even now, the memories feel inextricably linked: my vision problems, my parents' separation, and the new life Danny, Peter, and I would begin as we learned the divorce shuffle, living out of duffel bags as we ping-ponged our way be-tween our old house, now empty of the laughter and music that had filled it, and my mother's new one, which felt cold and for-eign. My brothers and I, always close, drew even tighter around one another. We were never alone, and we didn't talk about the divorce or about our feelings much, we just stuck together. We still argued: I took too long to get ready; Peter was bossy, always trying to parent us; and Danny was the loudest, always talking and singing, cracking us up even when he was irritating. But we were a team. Everything else might have been changing, but not the three of us.

If I had been given a choice then to have perfect eyes or my family back together, I would have picked the latter in a heart-beat. It was a much more devastating blow, even as I could feel my vision getting worse, and even though we were starting to notice, in what seemed to be an entirely unrelated problem, that I was having trouble hearing as well.

7

When my parents got separated and I was diagnosed with RP, they thought it would be best for me to start seeing a therapist. Not Dan or Peter, just me. Looking back I guess it made sense, but it confused me all the same. And it reinforced what I already believed to be true: I was the messed-up one. I was the one who was sneaky, who had a disability, who didn't do as well in school. I was the one who needed help, and I hadn't yet connected the help I needed to my disability.

Jamie's office was in a modern building above Market Hall in Rockridge, and I would sit in a big, comfy chair, trying to focus on anything but my parents' divorce—that's what I thought I was supposed to be talking about—and my thoughts would drift to the delicious food smells wafting up from the market. All I wanted to do was go downstairs to get a piece of the delicious focaccia I could smell. Why couldn't I be down there eating, or with my friends, or even home with my brothers, rather than sitting here alone in a room with a grown-up doing my best to talk about anything but my feelings?

So we made a deal. She would take me down and buy me focaccia, and then we would go back up to her office and I would talk to her. There was something about eating, and focusing on the food, rather than the emotions, that made it easier for me to talk. Sometimes we'd play board games, or I'd color, and she'd let me go through the toys she kept in her closet for younger children. I used my baby-talk voice, one that I used sometimes to avoid being serious, or because I wanted someone to like me and thought it might endear me to them.

Jamie was sweet and generous and listened to me attentively, her kind eyes never leaving my face. But I knew that I wasn't going to hold up my side of the bargain. I wasn't going to talk about my parents' divorce, or my eyes, or anything else that really mattered.

I wasn't going to say that I hated it when my mother asked us to make sure that Dad gave her that month's child support check, or that my dad would hand it to us impatiently and say, "Here, give this to your mother," as if that was all she was now, *our mother,* nothing to do with him. Or that I was angry with him for remarrying so quickly and didn't want to try to like my new stepmother.

I wasn't going to ask why it was just me sitting here, why they thought only I was fucked-up enough to need therapy.

I wasn't going to say that I despised the way that I sometimes caught my parents looking at me now, with worry or fear or sadness or some combination of the three that I couldn't quite discern.

No, I wasn't going to say any of that. I was just going to sit there, and eat my soft, fragrant bread, and find ways to ignore the giant elephants in every corner of the room.

8

I remember those sleepless nights each summer in June when my brothers and I had our trunks all packed, and we lay in bed tossing and turning, waiting for the clock to hit six A.M. so we could jump out of bed, drive to the bus, and head off to camp for another cherished summer. As a child, the day we left for Skylake Yosemite Camp was my favorite day of the whole year.

Skylake was one of the few things in my life that wouldn't change. Even after my parents' divorce, we were able to spend an entire month in one place, without having to bounce back and forth between houses. My life would simplify, as it did every summer: one cabin, a few bathing suits and sweatshirts, a simple day of fun and competition, swimming, campfires, dances, and, soon enough, kisses. I was just Becky there, not disabled or a child of divorce or a girl who needed a therapist.

As the bus drew closer to camp and passed through the last small town of Wishon, I craned my neck to see what was up ahead; it was so familiar that I seemed to know every tree. And then the trees would begin to clear and I would start to see glimpses of Bass Lake sparkling between them. I felt my body clench with excitement, while my brain started to relax to a safe, happy state, knowing I was going to the place where I felt most alive. The memories of my summers there are still ones that I use to access that place inside of myself where I feel like my truest, happiest self.

There was no better feeling than stepping off the bus and taking in that first deep breath of pine and pure, sweet mountain air, experiencing the chaos of searching for our friends, whom we looked forward to being with for the rest of the summer, and the yelling and screaming followed by adrenaline-filled hugs. Another summer at Skylake had begun.

One of my favorite things at Skylake was being awoken by the unique sounds of the birds early each morning. The first one awake, I would lie there listening for the sound of my favorite bird. Once she began to sing, her rhythm never changed. It seemed she was singing the words "But Beatrice." I knew it made no sense, but that was exactly what I believed the bird was singing. "But Beatrice!" (count to myself, one-two-three-four-five-six-seven-eight-nine-ten). "But Beatrice!" (one-two-three-four-five-six-seven-eight-nine-ten). "But Beatrice!". . . . It wasn't a pretty song. In fact, it sounded almost melancholy, but she was there every morning. She never failed me and she never missed a beat, and I always wondered who Beatrice was.

The recorded reveille bugle being played over the camp loudspeaker always interrupted the birds, and I remember how clear and crisp the first scratch of the needle put to the record sounded. I heard it with such ease. Back then I had no idea that in ten years I would not be able to hear the voice of a person standing directly in front of me. I could never have known how treasured this memory would become to me, waking up to the sounds of the earth.

9

When I was thirteen, my mother started noticing that I didn't answer her when she called for me from downstairs. At first she thought I was going through a teenage phase and didn't want to acknowledge her, but she soon started to worry. She said that the only time I seemed to respond was when she elevated her pitch to a high soprano singsong. So she went to the pediatrician and persuaded her to have my hearing screened. More tests. *Awesome.* Just what I wanted. She took me to the Children's Hospital in Oakland, where the top pediatric audiologist in the East Bay reassured her that the likelihood of my having hearing loss was slim. "Thirteen-year-old girls don't like to listen to their mothers," she maintained. But she promised to examine me thoroughly, as thoroughly as the eye doctors had, test after test. I could tell, though the doctors tried not to frown, that this was yet another test that I wasn't going to do well on.

What I knew: Apparently there was something wrong with my hearing, as well.

What I didn't know: When the doctor came out to talk to my

mother, all of the color had drained from her face, and she asked if she could run the tests again. When she returned, she gave my mother the good news—she had been worried that I had a brain tumor, but I didn't. The bad news—I had hearing loss. And though it was mild, right now, it was bilateral and symmetrical, meaning that it was affecting both ears. And, because of my eyes, she was worried that this was related and might be degenerative as well, and suggested that we see a geneticist.

The following month, my parents' worst fears were confirmed. I was indeed losing my hearing as well. The doctors couldn't tell them how quickly, but they knew that it was deteriorating, and that at some point I would be completely deaf. It was the first time, according to my parents, that the word "Usher" was used, even though the gene for Usher III had yet to be found.

The pain that my parents must have felt overwhelms me to this day. They had already gone through the heartbreak of learning about my eyes, and now, to learn that I was going deaf as well must have devastated them. I am convinced that it was even worse for them than it was for me, and I can only imagine what it must have felt like leaving that office. I hope that they were able to give each other even the smallest amount of comfort, to hug one another, and to promise that, even though we weren't a family anymore, we would face this as one. That's how I like to imagine it.

Here's the tricky part, where my memory, so sharp in some places, fades. I didn't know, truly did not know, until six years later, on that freezing winter's day in Michigan, the full extent of what was happening to me. I am sure that they told me, or told me most of it, but when I heard the word "Usher" at nineteen, it was foreign to me, an entirely new land. I knew that I had a degenerative eye disorder. I had hearing aids. How could I *not* have known?

I can think of all kinds of reasons, but what I come back to is this: I did not want to know. I was still a child, and I could not fathom it. A teenager, in my experience, can barely see a week into the future. What could years away possibly have meant to me? How could I really notice the incremental trickling away of my sight and hearing? The lengths to which we will go to not hear what we do not want to know are astounding.

10

My father and his second wife, Polly, met and married quickly, set up by a friend over nothing more than a fierce love of golden retrievers, baseball, and the Oakland A's. We were all still reeling from the divorce; as far as we knew my parents had been trying to "work it out" ever since the separation. I was Polly's maid of honor, wearing a Laura Ashley dress—think flowery bedspread with an oversized doily around the neck—and the ceremony, uncomfortably enough, was in the backyard of the house where we had once all lived together, back when we were a real family. The house where my mother had sung as we gathered around the piano, where she had cooked her signature spaghetti dinners, where we had congregated around the Thanksgiving table, lost our first teeth, taken our first steps. I stood next to Polly, who was straight-backed and beaming in a slim-fitting, knee-length dress that only someone with her figure could pull off, my eyes sweeping over the backyard where my father had stood countless times over the barbecue, grilling salmon or burgers and hot dogs. The same place where he had lifted Peter and Daniel and me in his arms, swinging each of us around until we were light-headed and screaming with dizziness and delight. I was heartbroken and bewildered, as children so often are, by how much was completely beyond my control and how all this could have happened. I looked down at my flowery dress while they said their vows, occasionally glancing at Daniel and Peter to see if they looked any happier than I felt. They didn't.

Soon after, we all spent our first weekend together as part of my father's new family. It was also the first time I saw snow. My dad and Polly were taking us to Tahoe, though none of us had ever been skiing before. I already hated the idea. The warmest piece of clothing I owned was a thick hooded sweatshirt with the logo of the University of Michigan, my father's alma mater, across the chest, but Polly cheerfully outfitted us in ski clothes and puffy parkas and packed us all into the car. I sat squished between Daniel and Peter in the backseat, closing my eyes and wishing that when I opened them it would be my mother in the passenger seat, that she would start belting out show tunes and we'd all playfully join in, my brothers and father singing the low parts while I tried to hit the high notes with my mother. But when I opened them it was not my mother's slender shoulder that my father's hand rested on but Polly's; she was in the driver's seat, the seat my mother never took when my parents were in the car together. She caught my eyes in the rearview mirror and half turned with a grin, telling us how excited she was to be with us and to introduce us to the snow. I closed my eyes again.

"You're going to love skiing!" she exclaimed.

Somehow, though, I had a feeling that a sport requiring grace, coordination, and quick instincts—and being out in the freezing cold—was not something I was going to excel at.

I didn't see much on the drive up and was unusually sullen

and quiet. But when we got to the cabin and stepped out of the car and into the snow for the first time, I couldn't help but be awed by the huge white peaks against the impossibly blue sky, the snow making the sun seem brighter than I'd ever seen it. Daniel had never been in the snow before either, but with the instincts of a mischievous kid he instantly started gathering up handfuls of it and throwing snowballs at Peter and me. Our first snowball fight ensued, in our typical style, which meant that no one was giving up, no matter how pelted they got, and in no time we were rolling in the snow, shoving it in each other's faces and down the back of one another's sweatshirts.

When we were done, breathless and laughing, I looked up and saw my dad and Polly, still unloading the car, stopping to smile broadly at the three of us. I felt a pang of guilt for having this much fun without my mom being there and closed my eyes again, feeling the warmth of the sun hitting my face, not wanting to look at any of this and think about how much and how quickly my life had changed.

The next morning I pulled out my bulky ski wear and began to layer on what felt like an absurd amount of clothing. Polly had lent me some of her things, but since she weighed about a hundred pounds soaking wet, and I was already bigger than that, the clothes felt both too puffy and too tight. By the time I clomped into the dining room to meet everyone for breakfast I felt like the Stay Puft Marshmallow Man and was ready to go back to bed.

Polly had been an avid skier for years and was so genuinely excited to be doing this with us that some of her enthusiasm started to rub off during breakfast. Maybe, I thought, as we walked outside and were greeted by a bright blue, cloudless sky, it wouldn't be so bad. Polly patiently had us fitted for boots and skis, checking each one of us, making sure we were comfortable and that our straps and snaps were properly done. By the time we were actually ready to ski it felt like hours had gone by, and then of course I had to pee, like I always do, which required an immense amount of work between the parka and the ski bib and trying to walk around in those ridiculous boots.

Finally we got to the gondola, and, as I freaked out about putting my skis in the ski rack and getting into the gondola in time, Daniel hopped right in next to Polly. Polly was a serious runner and an excellent athlete, and she and Daniel loved to compete and race one another; it was often too close to call a winner. There was no question, from the first time that Daniel stepped into his skis, that he was going to be awesome on the slopes. And it was clear that Polly was looking forward to having him pick up skiing quickly so that he could join her on the more challenging black-diamond runs. She showed us the first simple moves, and Daniel executed them expertly.

As in everything, Peter was a studious and diligent skier. He took his time but steadily made his way down the mountain, rarely losing the perfectly paralleled form of his skis. On the more difficult slopes he was careful, never falling and learning the rhythms of skiing, letting Polly and Danny race each other to the bottom of the mountain but quickly becoming competent.

Meanwhile, Dad and I were clearly far less coordinated than the rest of them, and generally wary of the entire sport. So, while Polly taught Daniel and Peter, Dad and I signed up for a beginner ski class. We awkwardly stumbled our way over to the bunny slope, made even clumsier by our bulky clothes, skis and poles jutting out from our sides in all different directions. I felt especially idiotic because I was wearing an old blue one-piece snowsuit of Polly's, complete with a rainbow across the back, so different from the stylish women skiing by me in their fitted

North Face jackets and Burton ski pants. Our ski instructor's name was something like Dale or Chad, an interchangeable ski-dude name, I would learn, and when he lifted his sunglasses off his face he displayed a raccoon tan the likes of which I never would have believed was possible.

Dale or Chad instructed us "dudes and dudettes" to get in line next to the pulley circuit, where we would wait for each one to come around for us, then grab on to it and let it pull us to the top of the hill. As each pulley came around, I thought to myself that they looked like rubber chickens, and I tucked my head into my chest and laughed to myself just long enough to miss mine and barely grab on to the next one. Mortified, I held on with all I had, but I didn't know how to prevent my skis and my legs from separating further and further apart from one another and before I knew it, I was in a deep split with my face planted in the snow and my butt in the air. Dale or Chad yelled for the operator to stop the circuit of rubber chickens so he could make his way up the hill to help me back up. As he effortlessly ran up the hill in his ski boots, his sun-kissed hair flowing behind him, yelling something that I couldn't hear, my dad clumsily attempted to traverse his way over to me from where he stood at the top of the hill to help. Unfortunately, he, too, lost his balance and fell over, so the whole group waited and watched as this father-daughter spectacle slowly maneuvered its way back onto its four useless feet.

This was pretty much how the morning went, and when we all finally met up at the lodge for lunch, I felt like I had been to war, and lost. The lodge was warm and smelled like French fries, and I decided that I was done with skiing and the snow for the rest of the day and would stay right where I was. Dad agreed, and after lunch, when Polly, Daniel, and Peter enthusiastically jumped back up, Dad and I drank hot chocolate and people-watched for the rest of the long afternoon.

Apparently, Polly and my brothers were having so much fun that they stayed until the last possible minute, and by the time they got back to the lodge to get us the gondola had stopped running, and the only way to get down the mountain to the village was by skiing down a blue-square slope called Village Run. The sun was starting to fall below the trees and the wind was picking up, and as we all walked outside I looked up at the sky nervously. It was already hard for me to see at dusk, and I was clearly a useless skier, so Polly decided that the only way for me to get down before the sun set completely was by having me ski in tandem with her, with me in front and between her legs.

I'm sure it's not easy for any kid whose parents have recently divorced to love her new stepparent. And I could not have been more embarrassed or looked more ridiculous, having this slender, competent woman spooning me from behind, our skis both in the classic "pizza wedge" beginner's move as we slowly made our way down the mountain, with even the six-year-olds effortlessly whizzing by us. But as it got colder and darker and much harder to see, Polly began to feel more solid to me. She was a real person, a permanent part of my life now, and I realized that I felt safe with her.

11

One warm June evening when I was fourteen Dad, Polly, and my brothers and I sat down to dinner. Polly had made us pasta, as usual. The country was in the midst of the pasta craze. It was before low-carb diets were on the radar, and everyone was convinced that low-fat, high-carb diets, the staple of the long-distance runner, were the way to go. Oh, if only that had been true. Polly had been handed three constantly hungry teenagers to feed and invested in a thick cookbook full of pasta recipes, and each night we'd joke around the table about whether we were eating pasta number 128 or pasta number 215. My dad sat at the end of the table with the top few buttons of his work shirt unbuttoned and his sleeves rolled up carelessly as we ate. Our three golden retrievers, Cubbie, Renner, and Star, lay outside, just behind the French doors that led to our yard, their big brown eyes staring at me with longing, wanting nothing more than to come gobble up whatever we (mostly me) had managed to spill and to lie at our feet. I already knew that when I had my own dog I would have no such rules; I'd never be able to resist those eyes.

My eyes were quickly diverted from dog watching and back to the table when my dad said, "Polly and I have special news to share with you guys . . ." By this time, I was not a big fan of "special news" or surprises, given all of the unanticipated news I'd received over the past several years, but I could tell right away that this was different. They were both smiling widely as my dad told us, "Polly is pregnant and we're having a baby."

Though it had been hard to accept a stepmother into my life, I was thrilled at the idea of a baby, and at being able to take care of a little brother or sister. "Are we going to find out the sex of the baby? When can we find out the sex of the baby? Do we know what we're going to name the baby? Can we help choose a name for the baby?" I asked in a rush. The thought of having a sister brought waves of excitement over me, and I became instantly convinced that it was all I had ever wanted. Later, though, as I lay in bed, other thoughts crept in. I wasn't sure what it all meant. Were Dad and Polly going to have a family of their own? Would we be included? How would our lives change? My dad had always been there for me: He would enlarge every paper and textbook page on his photocopier at work so that I could read them, advocating for me, always offering to help with anything that I was having trouble with. Would I still be his little girl? But the idea of having a younger sister kept breaking through these doubts, and I thought over and over to myself, *Let it be a girl, let it be a girl. . . .*

Three or four months into Polly's pregnancy, I was sitting in my eighth-grade algebra class, willing the clock to move faster. I hated math and science, and they always felt twice as long as my English classes, which would fly by, because there was nothing that I loved more than reading and writing. Then there was a knock on the classroom door, and Francine, the middle school secretary, stepped in and whispered something in my teacher's ear.

"Rebecca, your dad is on the phone and waiting to speak with you. Please go to the office." At first I was not as surprised about having to take the phone call as much as I was at having my prayers answered, but my steps slowed as I neared the office, wondering what he could be calling for. I was sure it couldn't be good. When we got back to the office Francine handed me the phone, and my hesitant "hello" was met with the eager enthusiasm of my dad's voice. "Rebecca Ann"—this is what my dad called me when either I was in trouble or he was reporting serious news to me—"you're going to have a sister!" I couldn't believe it. Finally, at fourteen years old, I was going to have a little sister! I was grinning from ear to ear when I returned to algebra and was completely unable to focus for the rest of class. Would she look like me? Would she share my brothers' and my goofy sense of humor? She would love them, but I was sure she was going to look up to me most of all. I would teach her everything that cool big sisters teach little sisters, and she would think I was so awesome.

I was so excited during the pregnancy that I wanted to spend lots of time with Polly, and this was when we first grew close. At night, after I'd finished my homework, I'd lie on their bed next to her to brainstorm names for the baby, laying my hand or head on her belly to feel my little sister kicking. We taped up a list of names for all of us to look over and play around with. We all had names that we liked that were included on the list: Zoe, Whitney, Madison, Caroline, Emily. Daniel came up with the name Sierra, which was generally a family favorite because we all loved the Sierra mountains. But Dad was worried that people would always mispronounce the name Sierra as "Sarah," so it never went far on the list of names. I came up with the name Lauren, which had always been one of my very favorite names for a girl. Until the day my sister was born, we still didn't know for sure what her name would be.

After a terribly long, drawn-out, and difficult delivery, Lauren Sierra Alexander was born on February 22, 1993. As it turned out, the woman who had just given birth in the room next to Polly had the last name of Sierra. We insisted that it had to be fate, and between that and Polly's horrific labor Dad finally gave in.

When I held her for the first time I felt so proud, as if I had helped to make her. The name I had wanted for her had been chosen, she was my little sister, and I would be able to do what I wanted to do most in the world: take care of someone else.

12

In February of 2013, I got a call from my junior high school alma mater, the Head-Royce School. They wanted me, in their one hundred twenty-fifth year, to be their distinguished alumna of the year. Which was very flattering but also somewhat surprising (and ironic), because when I was in the eighth grade, one of the high school deans at Head-Royce sat my parents down and explained to them that the school really couldn't "meet the needs of [their] daughter's disabilities" anymore. So I left, while Danny and Peter remained there until they had both graduated from high school.

Now, even though I had only graduated from their middle school and not their high school, they considered me an excellent alum, and a distinguished one, complete with Ivy League degrees and an inspiring piece on the *Today* show. I accepted, and admittedly a part of me hoped that Head-Royce would acknowledge their unwillingness at the time to accommodate my needs so that I could continue there for high school. More important, I hoped that after having me come and speak, they'd be open to giving the next student who needed extra accommodations a chance, and that person would someday be able to stand where I was and say, with all honesty, that this was the place that made it possible for them to be who they were today.

. . . .

Honestly, at the time, I felt mostly relieved to be moving to a new school, a school that was bigger and more diverse. For the first time, I was ahead in my schoolwork and finally got a chance to fully get a handle on my academics, buckle down, and get really good grades. I had never excelled at Head-Royce, which was a small, extremely academically driven private school. Somehow the combination of changing schools and finding out about my disabilities made me want to do well, *need* to do well, and for the first time in my life I started to push myself academically. It felt great to look down at the questions on a test and know that I was going to nail them, and I loved the satisfaction of getting something back with a big, fat red A on it.

It felt especially great because I had already learned that there were a lot of tests that I was going to fail, and even though it wasn't my fault, it upset me all the same. I knew by now that any test that took place in the doctor's office wasn't going to go well, and out on the soccer field, I wasn't going to be a star anymore—not even close.

There was something about hearing the words "On your marks . . . Get set . . . *Go!*" that created such a rush of energy and adrenaline in me that to this day, even hearing those words brings up feelings of nervous excitement. I remember racing other classmates on the playground of my elementary school when I was a little girl, feeling the rush of wind and hearing the other kids around us yelling and cheering us on as we ran. I used my arms to propel myself forward just like I saw the football players do on television, when they were running to score a touchdown. I ran as fast as I could, determined to be the first one to hit the wall with my hand, to be the winner. I wanted to be the fastest girl in my class just like Daniel was the fastest boy. Most important, I felt so alive, so free and empowered, even at seven or eight years old. I recognized my strength and ability and I loved nothing more than using it. There were a lot of things that I knew I did wrong—like lying—but I prided myself on my strength and coordination. I knew if I tried hard enough, I could win.

When I started my new high school, one renowned for its strong sports teams—especially girls' soccer—I wanted more than anything to be on the varsity team. I love to compete: I was always one of the kids picked first to be on a team, and when I came onto the field the girls on the other team would nudge each other and nod toward me, knowing that I needed to be guarded. I relished the butterflies and uncertainty at the beginning of a game, and I always played to win. I would race down the soccer field knowing that I could outrun my opponent and that I was in complete control of the ball. The goalie would see me coming and get ready, focus with all she had, but I knew I was going to get it in. Not necessarily because I was the best, but because I wanted it the most.

I'd been playing soccer my whole life, and I knew I was good, despite my disabilities. What I hadn't realized was that going from a small private school to a large high school would show me just how little the pond I'd been swimming in had been. So when I arrived for the first day of soccer tryouts in high school, I was confident, until I realized what "good" really meant. I suddenly became keenly aware of all of the things the other players could do that I couldn't—juggle a soccer ball, see the entire field as they dribbled the ball down it, and play just as aggressively when the afternoon sun was replaced by the evening dusk and it became more difficult to follow the ball.

Needless to say, I didn't make the varsity soccer team. I knew I wasn't as quick or skilled as the girls on the varsity team, but I still held out hope that somehow one of the coaches would see that, considering my visual limitations, I was a damn good player, and that that might make a difference. So I played junior varsity for my freshman and sophomore years of high school before I quit altogether. I was too embarrassed to be a junior in high school and still on the JV soccer team. Hadn't those years given me enough time and practice to become worthy of playing on the varsity team? Why couldn't I just try a little harder, be a little better, scan the field just a little faster? I was still giving it everything I had, but it wasn't enough.

Despite the fact that I was now excelling in school, I wanted to do more, be more, than I was right now, to find a way to fill the void that losing so much, and knowing I would lose so much more, had left in me. For the first time, too, I started to see beyond my own little world. Maybe I had a better understanding of the impermanence of things than many of my peers did. My world had changed so quickly—my eyes, the divorce, Polly, a new school away from my brothers—that I understood at a young age that there were many things that I wasn't going to be able to control, that were out of everyone's control. I couldn't change what was wrong with me, but I started to think about something that my father had taught me, that sometimes the best way to help yourself is by helping others.

As early as I can remember, my father instilled in us the importance of giving back to the community and to the world. There is a Hebrew word, "*tzedakah*," that translates as "righteousness" or "justice." It is generally used synonymously with "charity," but what it really means is a balancing of the scales—that charity is not an act of pity, or mercy, or even necessarily goodness, but of justice. You give back to make the world a better, fairer place— when you have an abundance, you share with those who have less. This was always an idea that resonated very strongly with me, though I have always had a much easier time giving help than accepting it.

My father led by example. Not only was he a leader and activist in our community, but he would put everything on the line for something he believed in. In 1984, a man named Kevin Cooper was sentenced to death for the brutal murder of four members of a white family. Cooper had just escaped from a minimum-security prison where he had been serving time for a nonviolent crime. He was found and charged, though the evidence was scant and many believed the trial was a sham, and spent the next twenty years on death row. During those two decades, Cooper, who always maintained his innocence, became an accomplished painter, writer, and speaker, and gained a huge following of people, organizations, and celebrities who believed that he was innocent, and, as the day of his execution grew nearer, the groups rallied together. My father, a corporate lawyer at a big firm at the time, took on the case, pro bono, and, leading a team of lawyers, got a stay of execution granted, ultimately going all the way to the Supreme Court to have it upheld. When his law firm had a conflict of interest with the case, he chose to leave it and pursue justice.

I wanted to be like my father and to reach out to help others. When I was fifteen, in the early nineties, after being extraordinarily moved by a young HIV-positive man named Scott Fried who came to speak at my synagogue, I began volunteering for Project Open Hand, a nonprofit organization delivering meals to people living with HIV/AIDS throughout the Bay Area. I wanted to know that I was making a real, tangible difference in people's lives, and I learned at an early age that knowing that I was helping someone else gave me great pleasure and a sense of purpose. I don't know whether or not my disabilities contributed to that feeling, whether I knew on some level that I was going to be someone who would need help more and more as my life went on, but it was something that was really important to me.

When I first started delivering meals, I didn't know what to expect. Perhaps that I would go in, chat, help in any way I could. Most people I delivered to, though, would talk to me through the door and ask me to leave the food on their doorstep, or they would open the door just wide enough so they could take the food we delivered to them. They generally didn't show their faces or want to be seen. It was in the early nineties, and there was still a terrible stigma around the disease, even in the Bay Area, and many of them may have been too sick to want anyone inside. It broke my heart to think of them alone with their pain and illness, feeling shut out from the rest of the world.

When I was seventeen, my father nominated me to run with the Olympic torch as a "community hero," and he submitted an application through *Sports Illustrated* to the Olympic committee about my work with Project Open Hand and my disabilities. I had no idea, and when they called I thought it was a prank. At first I was embarrassed. I wanted to be known as someone who helped others, but I didn't want to be known as someone who did this "even though she was disabled." I got over it quickly though, because how often do you get to run with the Olympic torch? There was a story about it in our local paper, and I ran holding the torch for almost a mile (it's heavier than it looks), my escort runner beside me, a motorcade behind me, crowds of friends and strangers lining the route and cheering me on.

13

There were things that I could do like any other normal teenager, that I didn't have to feel insecure or different about, and my absolute favorite was driving. When I was sixteen my sight was good enough to take the driving test, and my ophthalmologist assured me that it was all right for now, as long as I didn't drive at night.

I have always loved driving, and I was always excellent at it, as I still tell everyone who will listen, repeatedly. Though it's been years since I've been behind the wheel, I want them to know. Because of all the things I've lost, it was, in many ways, the hardest. As a teenager, there was nothing I was more excited about than getting my license, the ultimate ticket to independence. My dad was with me the morning I went to the DMV to take my test (which I passed with flying colors), then I dropped him off at the BART station and drove to school for the very first time by myself. I promised him that I wouldn't turn the radio on, and I was true to my word, completely focused and hyperaware of everything around me, so thrilled to finally be the one behind the wheel.

Sometimes I'd take the long route home from school to pass by as many after-school hangouts as I could, so that kids who knew me would see me driving. At school, I'd walk onto campus in the mornings, trying to look cool and collected while twirling my keys in my hand, hoping that the jingling would attract attention, and if anyone noticed I could say, "Oh, these? These are just my car keys. I almost forgot I had them in my hand!" Why I thought this would totally wow people I'm not sure, but I was convinced that it made me exponentially cooler and more desirable.

I'd head into homeroom, slide into a chair and drop my car keys with a big clank on the desktop in front of me, wait for my name to be called for roll, then take my sweet time putting them away in my backpack. For effect, I may have even struggled a little to find the right place to put them so that it would be clear to my classmates exactly what I was doing. I'm sure I looked like a total dork, but it was my first step toward real independence, and I relished it.

If not being able to drive at night was hard, giving it up altogether was wrenching. I had already moved to New York, a city made for pedestrians—half the people I know who grew up in the city don't drive—and part of the reason I chose New York was so that I wouldn't stand out so much or feel so needy. For all of its craziness, New York is a wonderful city for pedestrians. But to lose the freedom of driving, the joy that being behind the wheel gave me, the concrete evidence of my independence, devastated me. I can admit now that I drove long past when I should have stopped.

One of the last times I drove, when I was twenty-seven, is one of my most vivid memories. I was cruising back to the city from the Hamptons, alone in a convertible with the top down, singing along enthusiastically to the radio. I felt totally free, and loved the faint smell of the ocean and the feeling of the wind whipping through my hair. I wanted so badly to just keep on driving and to just say the hell with this, I am not letting this be taken away from me, too, not this. When I visit my family in California I ache to drive along the beautiful redwood trees that line the curvy roads of Highway 17 to Santa Cruz, or to cruise down the Pacific Coast Highway, watching the crashing waves below as I expertly navigate the turns, totally confident in myself.

I've promised myself that I won't dwell on what I've lost—it's a waste of time, and I know just how precious time is. So I try not to mourn it, but instead to look back and see that girl, the one with the wind blowing through her hair, feeling so completely independent—so alive and free—and to know that she is still inside of me, and that this is a memory that will stay with me, stay part of me, forever. For me, memories of things I have lost or can no longer do are incredibly vivid, almost like I could step right back into them, as though the past were right here next to the present. We all lose things, and I will suffer far worse losses. We all will. I have only one choice, and that is to keep on living while looking forward to what is ahead, rather than back at what has been lost. Helen Keller once said, "What we have once enjoyed we can never lose. All that we love deeply becomes a part of us." I try every day to remember that, because I need that to be true for me.

But, just so you know, I was an excellent driver.

14

Another thing that really helped to normalize high school for me was my boyfriend Cody. When I first met him, at sixteen, it was at the party of a mutual friend. He was there with my friend Dan and sat in the corner, goofing off and making fun of people. I figured he was an asshole, and when I came over to say hi to Dan, Cody was obnoxious enough that I ignored him for the rest of the evening, even when he later tried to talk to me. We moved in the same wide circles and kept running into each other after that, and, even though I thought he was a jerk, he was growing on me. One night he decided to prank-call me, and it was annoying and dumb, but it was funny, the equivalent of young boys on the playground, chasing and pinching girls in a clear bid for their attention. I soon realized that he wasn't who I had first pegged him to be.

Funny and often sweet, with an offbeat sense of humor that matched mine, he was the most hilarious person I knew. Cody was tall and fit, with beautiful hazel green eyes and an adorable smile. It never occurred to me to hide my disabilities from him, either. It just didn't matter to him. When I got my first hearing aid I refused to wear it and would only grudgingly agree to put it on during AP history, where our teacher was a low-talking mumbler whom everybody had difficulty understanding. I would slip it into my ear, making sure that it was carefully covered by my hair, and take it out the moment class was over. I wasn't embarrassed in front of Cody, though, and later, when my hearing loss had progressed, he was the one who encouraged me to wear my hearing aids. I didn't realize that I could come off as rude, as though I was ignoring people when I just couldn't hear them. Cody told me this, without judgment, and could even joke with me about it.

He was also my first real love. We waited a long time to have sex—seven months, which felt like forever as teenagers—but by the time we did, we knew each other's bodies so well, and were so comfortable with one another, that it felt completely natural. I learned with him where I liked to be touched gently and where I preferred the feeling of firm hands on my body. Feeling the brief wisps of air that passed over us as we moved together reminded me of how freeing it felt to be exposed. Cody's warm breath against my ear, down my neck, to my collarbone as his hand rested on my bare hip sent a tingling sensation throughout my body. This was possible because nothing between us was forced—my trust in him invited his touch. I felt so safe with my body in his hands and protected by how close his skin was to mine.

I learned so much about myself through physical touch. With him, I developed trust and confidence in my own body, and I learned to trust someone else with my body as well. I allowed myself to be vulnerable, to explore and be explored. This was my first true experience with intimacy that came from deep within me—a time when the strength of my relationship to someone emotionally enabled me to understand the vital connection between trust and touch.

. . . .

I remember one night when Cody and I were lying in his room, and the only light coming in was from the streetlamp through his window. I could see his silhouette, lying next to me as he traced my face with his fingertips, and then, when he stood up I saw his shadow on the floor, outlined by the moonlight. I remember being surprised that I could see it at all and feeling so lucky that I could. Kids are so fascinated by their shadows. How they lengthen and shorten, and how when they're long they can look almost as tall as their parents. I knew already that shadows were something that would be completely gone soon.

15

When I landed it felt like an explosion. I don't remember the pain, just trying to rasp out a yell, but all that came out was the faint cry of a wounded animal.

I had gotten drunk enough that night that Cody was angry with me. It was one of our last hurrahs the summer after high school, and everyone was psyched to be out, the night full of promise and nostalgia. We were all headed off to college in the fall. Daniel and I were going to the University of Michigan together, and I couldn't wait to be with him after four years at separate schools. Cody and I knew that we didn't have much more time together, which made him even more pissed that I had ruined the night. Dancing was one of our favorite things to do, and we were going to a hip-hop club. Cody was a great dancer, and there was nothing as fun for the two of us as being on the dance floor together.

. . . .

I love to have a good time. I'm prone to laughing at inappropriate times and swearing too much, and I have absolutely always loved to dance and to sing. My brothers and I loved to perform. We played the piano and were always in the school musicals. When I was younger and my hearing was still strong enough to clearly hear all of the words, I loved to make up my own choreography to my favorite songs, and my friends and I would spend hours creating intricate dance routines. As I became a teenager I started listening to all kinds of music: hip-hop, rap, classic and alternative rock. There was nothing I loved more than the sound of a good beat.

I adored camp and school dances: My friends and I would listen eagerly to hear which song would be played next, and when one of our favorites came on we would yell and scream with excitement, singing along while waving our arms in the air and throwing our hair around. I loved, too, the moment when a slow song would come on, the first strains of it sending my stomach into knots as I wondered who might ask me to dance.

I believe that dancing is one of humanity's greatest gifts. It allows you to feel and express so many different emotions. When you see someone dancing without inhibition, no matter how silly or outrageous they might look, one thing is certain: They are truly living in the moment. Nothing feels better to me than my body matching the rhythm of a song; I might not be able to make out the lyrics anymore, or sometimes even the tune, but I don't need my eyes and ears to feel the bass pounding through me, and I don't need to see or hear well to dance. When I first hear or feel music, a signal goes right to my shoulders, and before I know it I am well on my way to starting a dance party.

. . . .

That night, though, before we went to the club we had been hanging out in a park nearby, passing a bottle of Smirnoff, which

Daniel's girlfriend Lesley and I drank most of. I was always a light-weight and never much of a drinker, so by the time we made it into the club and onto the dance floor I was starting to feel the effects. I went to the bathroom and could tell by my wavy reflection that I was wasted. Within minutes, I was stumbling, unable to dance or even form a coherent thought. The bouncer had his eye on me and soon asked my friends to get me out of there. Cody and Daniel practically had to carry me out, and, even though I was totally out of it, I could see that Cody was angry. He wouldn't talk to me on the ride home, and didn't say good-bye when we dropped him off, and that's the last thing I remember, though Lesley told me later that she had walked me upstairs and gotten me into bed. I woke up several hours later, around four thirty A.M., still drunk and desperate to pee and get some water, and stumbled out of bed.

I still don't know if what happened next was from the booze or my degraded vision, or, most likely, some combination of both. My night vision already sucked, and I couldn't see a thing as I lurched out of bed. I felt my way along the wall, struggling to find my door, but I was so disoriented that I had no idea where it was. I started to panic and moved more frantically, my drunk brain unable to help me find even this most familiar of routes. I fumbled by my French windows—I don't know if I actually turned the big handle to open them or whether they had already been open, but as I became more and more turned around, desperate to get out of my room, I managed to back up against my large, open window (honestly, I think I might have been trying to sit down on the ledge, perhaps thinking I had finally found the toilet) and fell backward more than twenty-seven feet onto the flagstone patio behind our house, landing, miraculously, on my left side, breaking almost everything but my head and neck. Mere inches and my story would have ended right there.

I don't know how long I lay there, probably only a minute or two, but even my quiet wails were becoming too much for me when, in an extraordinary stroke of luck, a neighbor who lived behind us, a cop just getting home from a very late shift, heard me. He ran across the street to look over the wall behind our house and then raced to me. How my mother heard me I still don't know, but with the keen sense that only a mother has, she instantly woke up and came into my room. When she didn't see me she raced frantically through the house, trying to follow my voice, and then ran back to my room in frustration, and this time noticed the gently blowing curtain and the wide-open window. She looked out and saw me splayed across the flagstones. By the time she got to me our neighbor was there, making sure to keep my neck and head still, the ambulance on its way.

When the EMTs and police got there they were sure that I must have jumped or that my mother had pushed me. I wanted to explain, but my voice wasn't working, and my body was in total shock. But I knew what they must have been thinking. How on earth could someone fall out a window?

I still couldn't feel anything below my neck, but that would come soon enough, an unimaginable pain, every inch of me burning like it was on fire. I was rushed to the trauma center at Highland Hospital in Oakland, which was generally reserved for gunshot wounds from drive-by shootings. I lay on the gurney, croaking out profuse apologies and attempting to assure anyone who would listen that I was sorry to have caused them so much trouble, that I was really okay. They looked at me as though I was insane, because I was not remotely okay. Every limb on my body was broken in some form: My entire left foot was completely shattered, as were my left hand and wrist; my right hand was broken; and one of my vertebrae was fractured and compressed.

Ultimately, the only thing left without a cast would be my right leg and foot.

A nurse came over and introduced herself, explaining that she was clipping off my ring because my body was swelling up so fast. Cody had given it to me, and I was devastated, tears coming for the first time and streaming down my cheeks. I hadn't yet comprehended what devastating shape I was really in; all I could focus on was that ring, and I was heartbroken. *Is Cody still mad at me?* I wondered, with the idiocy that only a teenage girl could possess.

They transferred me as quickly as they could to Alta Bates hospital in Berkeley, the same hospital where I had been born, where I would spend the next month.

The first operation I would have would be reconstructive surgery on my shattered left foot and hand, but it had to wait at least a week, to give the massive swelling time to go down. Those days passed in a miserable opiate haze, the pain so excruciating that when I came up from it even a little I was instantly given more morphine, and it took weeks to wean me from it. The nurses had given me a clicker so that I could administer my own morphine when I felt I needed more. It looked like something you might see on *Jeopardy!* for contestants to click as soon as they have an answer for Alex Trebek, and I was convinced that it was some kind of psychological prop that they used to keep the patients from screaming at them for more meds, because I would click that button with my thumb over and over again to no avail and have to call them anyway. I guess I was one of the ones in bad enough shape that they always came running when I needed them, which I'm sure was often, as I have been told many times by my mother that the morphine made me behave like a total maniac and rendered me completely incapable of reason or grace.

I was also unable to move in my hospital bed without the help of several nurses. Since I was completely immobile they would come in every few hours to adjust my body so that I wouldn't get bedsores, which was a nearly impossible job for them. They couldn't actually pick me up or move my limbs because of the severity of my injuries, so they had various methods of moving me with the use of pillows. Even the tiniest of movements would make me scream in pain, and the catheter that I had to use left me with the constant, urgent feeling of needing to pee. I cringe now, thinking of how ungrateful I must have seemed, how unreasonable and crazy, between the pain and my drug-induced delirium. I had always prided myself on being polite to a fault, but now I could barely recognize my old self. In a matter of seconds my life had changed completely, from being a babysitter chasing after little kids, so excited to go off to college and be independent and have what felt like my "real life" begin, to a patient stuck in this bed, lucky to be alive but totally incapacitated. I was completely dependent on others and in a kind of pain that I couldn't escape no matter how many drugs they pumped into me.

I was only given one task that week, and, strangely enough, it was the only thing that made life bearable. In order to make sure that the morphine wasn't suppressing my breathing too much, I had to blow into a small tube and make a miniature Ping-Pong ball rise in it with as much breath as I could muster, trying to get it to bob above a little blue line in the tube. It was my first challenge, and even pumped full of morphine I tried to focus everything I had on it. I was determined to make that ball rise all the way to the top, and I lay in my room blowing it as often as I had the strength, surrounded by bouquets of flowers and get-well balloons. At first I could barely get it to move, but I learned right from that first week that the only way to get through this was going to be to look at it as a challenge and give it everything I had. To take my shattered, drugged body and do what I could with it. I was going to blow the shit out of that ball, and everyone was going to be proud. I was going to ace the ball test like no one ever had before. I'd be in the books, the girl who blew the ball sky-high. I had worked hard in school, on the soccer field, in school plays, but this was so far beyond anything I had faced. I had no body, I couldn't move anything. The ball was it.

When people hear the story of my accident, the horror they feel is probably even worse than what it would be for someone else. "Oh my God, with everything else you've had to endure, how awful!" But I learned something integral to who I am today, who I've been able to become. The perseverance I would need every day of my life really began in that bed, with that little ball. The rest of the long, painful recovery would come, but I had already learned the lesson, that I had to meet it head-on, one day, one hour, one minute at a time. There was just no other way to do it. Every single thing that I have accomplished in my life that means something to me was done with really hard work, and the moment that started was there, in my hospital bed.

16

My first surgery lasted twelve hours. Two doctors took bone from my hip, each using some to reconstruct my left hand and foot, one starting as soon as the other had finished working on his respective appendage. I had two screws put into my left hand to hold everything together, and the bones in my left foot were shattered so far beyond recognition that it had to be completely rebuilt.

Before the surgery my parents had been told that some of the bone in my foot would have to be fused together, and that I would walk with a significant limp for the rest of my life and would probably never be able to run again. They made the wise decision not to mention this to me before my surgery.

After the surgery, as I lay in casts in the bed, the days passed by endlessly. The things that made me happy were such small ones, but I came to appreciate them so much. I would lie in the dark, generally awake before dawn, smelling the flowers that always filled my room (the nurses referred to my room as "the flower shop"). My grandma Faye gathered them from her garden and from her friends' gardens to bring to me when she drove up from Santa Cruz. The smell of the flowers masked many of the horrible medicinal smells of the hospital, which were so nauseating to my already heightened sense of smell. I spent hours lying incapacitated in my hospital bed watching the flowers bloom. Each morning I looked forward to seeing how much they had bloomed overnight. Unable to move most of my body on my own, the simple pleasure of watching them open gave me a sense of peace. I first experienced the beauty of stargazer lilies while I was recovering in the hospital, and they became my favorite flowers. Not only because of their bright color and fragrance, but because of how long they lasted and how significantly they changed size, color, and scent as they bloomed. I fell more and more in love with them as I watched the life cycle of each lily that kept me company in my room.

When that first light started creeping across the window I would be so overjoyed, knowing that someone would be there soon. In the beginning my family would take turns spending time with me, so I had someone there as much as possible. My parents, Polly, and Grandma Faye were frequent visitors and occasionally spent the night. Cody stayed over, but only once. I don't know if he blamed me for my accident or just didn't want his summer to be ruined spending it by my bedside when we both knew we'd be going our separate ways in the fall, but we were clearly over the night I fell out the window. Or over for the time being. Lots of friends came, too, but then summer plans and the excitement of getting ready for college came, and as they prepared to start their new lives, the visits and phone calls slowed to a trickle, and still I lay, unmoving, in my hospital bed.

Then one friend, Lisa D'Orazio, not a close friend but one I had always liked, surprised me by visiting one day. We had gone to high school together, but we weren't close, though I had always admired her. She was popular, a varsity soccer player hanging out with upperclassmen since freshman year, much cooler than I was. When she heard about the accident, though, she came to visit. Then she showed up again. And again, bringing me mix CDs of music that we both loved: Motown, old-school rap, and hip-hop. She would call, too, just to say hi, and to help to relieve the monotony of lying in my room all day.

She didn't act like she felt sorry for me; she really seemed to want to be there, and just having her come and hang out made such a difference. It was so generous, so kind of her, and I knew I wanted to be that person, that if someone I knew was lying immobile in a bed I could be thoughtful enough to do that. Just being there, or knowing that someone else is there for you, makes every difference. Lisa had no idea at the time how much she was doing for me, but it made us lifelong friends. She is one of my favorite people in the world, and I know we'll be there for one another no matter what.

I had a favorite nurse, Roberta, and I looked forward to the mornings, when she would be back. She would greet me with her wide smile and brusque kindness, and Roberta was the only nurse that I wanted to bathe me. Well, not bathe precisely. She would use warm washcloths to clean the parts of me that weren't casted, slowly tilting my head back into a warm basin of water to wash my hair, and then she would gently pat me dry. When Roberta couldn't do it, I wanted Polly. My stepmother, for the first time, was the person that I wanted most.

My parents, so loving and caring, were not what I needed right then. I did not want pity. I did not want to see their tears—more heartbreak and more worry, caused by me. Polly was what I needed. If there was anyone who was going to help me make damn sure that I got up and walked, it was my stepmother. She got shit done. She is kind, but she is also as no-nonsense as a person gets. She loved me, but she wasn't going to look down and see her broken stepdaughter, poor thing, who, in addition to having a devastating syndrome that would someday render her blind and deaf, might very well be left physically disabled. Nope. She was going to see Rebecca, who did not want to stay in this bed, did not want sympathy, and needed to get up as fast as was earthly possible and get to college, where she belonged.

As the doctors and the social worker discussed a possible discharge date for me, my parents decided it was time to tell me that I would not be able to attend college in the fall as I had planned. My injuries were simply too severe, they explained, and it would take me at least a year of physical therapy to become independent again. I was devastated. Though I should have realized that of course I wasn't going to be able to leave for Michigan anytime soon, I had felt like once I was out of the hospital the hardest part would be over, but that wasn't even close to true. My twin brother, my high school sweetheart, and all of my friends would be leaving to begin an exciting new chapter of their lives, while I stayed behind relegated to a wheelchair, working harder than I ever had in my life just to relearn the simple tasks that I had always taken for granted.

My back and all of my other limbs were broken and heavily casted, except for my right leg, and the hospital wouldn't discharge me until I could successfully sit up in bed, stand up, pivot myself to the side, and transfer myself into my wheelchair, all on my own. I needed to be able to do this with only the use of my right leg and then wheel myself out, propelling myself, again, just using that one leg. Needless to say, my right leg became my rock, and it gave me everything it had. I practiced every day, over and over again, until I was able to transfer myself three times in a row. I have never wanted to get out of anywhere as much as I wanted to leave that hospital room.

. . . .

I was so relieved to be going home, knowing that I was one step further in my recovery. We'd decided that I would live in the little guesthouse at Dad and Polly's, which would be easier because it had no real stairs for me to climb from the driveway. Actually, I'd decided. I wasn't ready to go back to my mother's house, the scene of the accident, and I refused to move back and forth between my parents' houses as I had been doing for so many years. Though it is really hard for me to upset people, and I didn't want to hurt my mother, this was one of the first times when I had to be firm and clear and put my wishes and needs above other people's feelings.

A friend of my family's who was big into dirt bikes very kindly offered to build a few wooden ramps for me to use, so that I could wheel myself from the driveway into the guesthouse and from the bedroom to the bathroom. He also made an extra ramp for me to use to get into my mom's house, for the day when I would be ready to return.

The ramp was my next challenge. It took me a few practice rounds to muster enough strength and force for my right leg to be able to hurtle me up to the top of the ramp in my wheelchair without my rolling backward right to where I'd started. Fortunately, it was challenges just like this one that I loved the most. Nothing made me happier than practicing something I struggled with until I'd mastered it. This would be the ongoing theme of my recovery; hard work was the only way I was going to get there.

It was the only way I was going to walk—normally, I was sure, despite what the doctors said—and it was the only way I was going to get back on track and move on to the life I was so desperate for. I knew there was no way I was going to college that fall, but I refused to believe it would take me a whole year to recover, so I set my sights on January. Then, I promised myself, I would be ready.

17

My new home consisted of a queen-size bed, with many pillows to help keep parts of my body elevated. In the beginning, Dad or Polly would come in the evenings to help arrange them so that I would be comfortable enough to sleep. On one side of the bed there was room for my wheelchair and enough space so that I could transfer myself in and out. On the other side, up against the bed, was a long table that held everything that I needed. My bed, the table, and my wheelchair became my humble little home for the next five months, everything I needed within grabbing distance.

Polly had given me a wall calendar filled with photos of puppies so that I could keep track of all of my doctors' appointments now that I was back at home. Even that small gesture from her, having me be the keeper and organizer of my own schedule, was important to me. So little was in my power, but she treated me like an adult, able to schedule and keep track of everything I needed to do for my recovery.

That very first night, as I lay there looking around my new

home, I saw a red Bic pen lying underneath the table and I decided that I needed it. As I checked out the small collection of items on my table, I decided that the best tool at my disposal would be my wooden back scratcher with the hand at the end that I used to scratch inside my casts. The pain was still terrible sometimes, but even worse was the itch. I already had an overly sensitive sense of touch, and scratching my itches was a feeling that verged on the celestial.

I was able to reach the pen with the scratcher to pull it closer to the bed, but I still had no way of reaching down and actually picking it up off the floor. I didn't want to have to wait until morning to ask someone to get it for me, so, with the help of my elbows, I scootched my way to the other side of the bed, put my right foot down on the floor, and pivoted my whole body just the way I'd practiced a gazillion times in the hospital before I was released.

With my right foot I pushed myself in my wheelchair around the bed as close to the table as I could. After I secured the brakes, I braced myself again with my elbows on the armrests of the wheelchair and stuck my right foot out as far under the table as I could. With a little maneuvering, I reached the pen with my foot and pulled it closer to me until I was able to pick it up with my toes and bring it to my hand.

I felt triumphant that I had found a way to do this all by myself, and I realized right then that this would be vastly different from my time in the hospital. I was not going to be lying around waiting for my broken body to heal, I was going to be the one to heal it. As I made my way back onto the bed, realizing for not the last time how grateful I was for my elbows, which were integral to everything that I could do at that time—not to mention my toes—I took the red pen awkwardly in my casted hand and crossed out the very first day of my recovery with a bold red X on my puppy calendar. This was why I had needed the pen. For the rest of my time in the guesthouse this would be the highlight of my day—crossing off another box on my calendar each night before I went to bed, counting down the days until my next doctor's appointment, follow-up surgery, or physical therapy appointment arrived.

The only thing worse than the itch was the boredom. My friends had gone off to college; I felt as though everybody's life had gone on without me, and I wasn't really in touch with any of them. It's so hard to remember now how different things were, but this was before the Internet, back when no one but high-powered businessmen carried a cell phone. Email had just been introduced, but dial-up was slow as molasses, and no one was using it much yet.

I still had visitors. My parents came all the time, bringing food and books and anything that I needed, staying for every hour that they could, and friends and family called occasionally. Lauren would come visit me, hoisting herself up onto my bed and talking on and on to me, distracting me from my boredom with her babbling. I was so desperate for company that I was even excited when a nurse from the Visiting Nurse Association came to the house to help bathe me every few days. When they didn't come, my grandma or Polly would help me. I'd wheel myself into the bathroom, put the lid of the toilet seat down, and then I'd transfer myself using my right leg to sit on a towel placed on top of it. I would sit there, naked but for my casts, passing a washcloth back and forth with whomever was there to help me that day. They would patiently wash every exposed inch of my body, and, while at first it was embarrassing, it was such a relief to be washed, and it felt so good to be clean.

Once a week I'd pull my wheelchair up to the sink and put my head back slightly while my helper used a cup to scoop water from the sink to wash my hair, massaging the shampoo deep into my scalp. That was the most wonderful feeling of all. With most of my body in casts, I felt as though so little of me was ever touched, and when it was, it was generally in a very clinical way. To have someone's hands touching me affectionately was such a relief and a joy. I longed to be able to throw my arms around someone for a hug, to snuggle, to dance up against Cody, even just to hold someone's hand.

Grandma Faye came to stay for a few weeks, arriving with armfuls of flowers, and, in addition to helping me bathe, she would spend long hours talking and visiting with me. I felt like I really got to know her at that time, as a person and not just a grandma, and I treasured our time together. She is still gorgeous, even now, at ninety-six, with beautiful, keen blue eyes and an infectious smile. Every day she completes the *New York Times* crossword puzzle. She travels the world on Road Scholar tours, is about to go to China and the Far East, and has remained a student of life for nine and a half decades.

When we spend time together now, both with our hearing aids, me with my cane and her with her walking stick, Grandma Faye is a living example of what she taught me then. Nobody wants to hear you complain, so keep the bitching and moaning to yourself. Embrace the world with a positive outlook, and you will get so much more out of life. She is such an inspiration to me, and she was indispensable to my recovery.

Even with my visitors, though, I spent most of my time alone. Although I used as many hours as I could to help myself recover, doing the exercises prescribed for me diligently, there always seemed to be more time. Waiting, waiting, waiting. As an adult, spending time alone is something I cherish. At that time, though, the loneliness was excruciating.

One night, when I didn't think I could take another minute of sitting in the bed, my family and I decided to go to the movies. I was so excited to finally be going somewhere, anywhere; it had been so long since I had done anything that would even remotely be considered fun. When we got to the theater, though, we found out that the movie we had come to see was all the way upstairs and not wheelchair accessible. As I looked up at the huge flight of stairs in front of me, which might as well have been Mount Everest, I felt completely defeated, my disappointment almost bringing me to tears. It was the first time I realized what a challenge even the simplest pleasure that we all take for granted could be for someone with disabilities, and it gave me an appreciation for what some people have to go through just to do things that most never think twice about. At the time, I didn't connect it with my other disabilities, but I would soon enough learn that feeling myself. We ended up at a Disney movie downstairs.

A month or so after my first surgery I had a follow-up one to take the metal pins out of my left foot. After so many surgeries I was terrified and exhausted by the idea of going back to the hospital—another cast, another recovery. Even though I would only have to stay over for one night this time, the idea of even another hour in one of those sterile, medicinal rooms made me nauseous. Then, though, I remembered the present Lisa had given me right before she had left for college.

Knowing that I had to go back in, she had made me a surgery CD, and as soon as they started prepping me the headphones went on. By the time they wheeled me into anesthesia they had already given me a little something, and I was singing along heartily to "Joy and Pain" by Rob Base; I conked out right in the middle of James Brown's "Get on Up." It was unbelievable that such a little thing made it all so much less scary and more bearable.

When the doctor finally removed the cast, it felt as though my leg and foot didn't belong to my body. Most of the bones in my foot were grafted from my hip, and I couldn't believe that it was mine. At first I was terrified to move it, sure that I would somehow damage it. My physical therapy began, three times a week, and I looked forward to those days more than anything. We would begin with my hand, for which I worked on range-of-motion exercises, followed by a session for my foot, still so fragile and tender. When they first put me on the stationary bike I could only do ten minutes because my leg was so weak, but as the weeks went on, and my body got stronger, I loved being on that bike.

Once I was finally in my walking cast I could drive myself to physical therapy, which felt like the sweetest taste of freedom. It was such a relief to be able to do something for myself, to be behind the wheel again, that I almost cried as I slid into the driver's seat for the first time.

I'd always been athletic, but after my accident I had lost a lot of weight, my left calf had atrophied, and my strong, sturdy body looked completely changed. It was the first time I became aware of the connection between my mind and my body, and taking care of it became a priority. It took the accident to make me realize just how crucial it was for me to pay attention to and care for my body. I felt the same way that I later would about my sight and hearing: that I had to appreciate my body for the gift that it was. It prepared me in ways for what was to come, and it helped me to realize just how resilient I was.

When I wasn't at physical therapy I worked to rehabilitate myself in the driveway, every minute that I had the energy for. I had never been so focused and driven. I still look back at that time to give me strength, knowing that, since I got through it, I could get through anything. My life was so stripped down that even the smallest movements became triumphs. I went from wheelchair to crutches—special ones, because both my hands were broken, and I couldn't put weight on them—and then I graduated to a walking cast and slowly began to bear weight, at last, on my left foot. Lauren would sometimes come play in the driveway while I was out there, running circles around me on her strong little legs, the excellent athlete she would one day be already starting to emerge, and I longed for the time when I took for granted all of my working parts, and prayed for a time when I might be able to again.

18

As I promised myself I would be, I was ready to begin college the winter after my accident. I knew I couldn't go all the way to Michigan, since I still needed to see my doctors frequently, and I feared that the snow and ice would be a real hazard for me. I had been admitted to UC Santa Barbara, and we decided that I should begin there and move to Michigan when my body felt ready.

I couldn't wait to go, to be out of the guesthouse and back in the world of the living, and it felt like ages since I had spent time with people my own age. Lisa was at UC Santa Barbara, as well, and I was psyched to find out that we were in the same dorm. Without hesitation she welcomed me into her circle of friends, wonderful women whom I am close with to this day.

Every day my body felt a little bit stronger. My friends and I would go to the gym together, and I appreciated it—even the StairMaster—more than I could have previously imagined. My friend Sophie and I would listen to the radio on our Walkmen, and when a song came on that we both loved we would look at each other, and, even if we were across the room from one another, we would burst simultaneously into loud song. It felt so good to laugh and sing with friends, and, best of all, I could finally dance again. My friends and I would have impromptu dance parties, music blasting from our dorm rooms, caught up in the joy of our newfound independence. There is something about singing and dancing with my girlfriends that is totally irreplaceable; it gives me a feeling of such delight and freedom to be in the middle of a throng of joyful, dancing bodies. Even the stupidest keg party was made fun as soon as a great song came on and we could take over whatever space there was to get our groove on. We would sing and dance everywhere we went, and I loved it all the more for having not been able to do it for so long. Already, the sunshine and work and fun of college were helping the months of being immobile fade from my mind, though the scars, and the pain, would remain.

. . . .

Chronic pain is an insidious thing. While my accident was certainly an important lesson in patience and perseverance, the physical pain won't ever be gone. My back, hand, and foot have never been the same, and while I have tried not to let it stop me from doing anything that I really want to, I struggle with it every day. Like my diminished vision and hearing, it is something that I will always have to live with. As with the tinnitus, I try to tune it out, and sometimes I can. It's amazing what the body can get used to. I try to keep it to myself, because, as Grandma Faye would say, nobody wants to hear it. Complaining has never gotten me anywhere, so I try my best not to.

19

The summer after the accident, when I was nineteen and had just finished my second quarter at UC Santa Barbara, I returned to Skylake Yosemite Camp as a counselor. Cody came with me. He was in college at San Diego State, and we had gotten together a few times that spring, making trips to visit one another, and were a couple again that summer. It felt almost like being resurrected to go back to my old life, but with a joy and appreciation I couldn't have imagined before. As happy as Skylake had always made me, to now be able to do things I thought I might never do again, to be fully alive and back in the world, made me happier than I had ever been. And to be with Cody again, though we both knew that it was only temporary, an interlude together between our own separate lives, felt good, familiar and comfortable and right.

It was the last summer I still had enough hearing to wake up to the sounds of birds. I could hear their individual songs, including the trill of my beloved Beatrice, though they were fainter, of course. The next significant decline in my hearing came just a few months later, and I would never again be able to hear my morning birds without my hearing aids. Even with them, my discrimination—which is another part of hearing loss, being able to distinguish similar sounds from one another—would never be good enough again to hear them distinctly.

I was a swim counselor, my eyes and ears still strong enough to scan the water for any signs of trouble. Shallow nineteen-year-old that I was, I had mostly requested swimming because I wanted to be on the docks next to the water so I could work on my tan, but it turned out that I also loved to swim. The coolness calmed the ache in my foot and felt wonderful on my mostly recovered body. Swimming was exercise that was demanding without being painful, and it was that summer that I really felt my body come fully back to life.

Each morning I woke early, before reveille; put on my bathing suit; and left my hearing aids behind. I'd head down the swim trail to the still silent, empty lake—no screaming kids or boats roaring yet—where the water was still calm, and you could see just the gentlest ripple as the water lapped lazily at the rocks along the tip of the shore. I would slip in, the first to break the stillness, the lake all mine. I didn't need my eyes and ears then, just the warmth of the water—strangely balmy in the morning, while it was icy cold during the day—embracing me, the clean scent of the lake and the trees, and, most of all, the feel of my body, every muscle and tendon waking.

I had always loved competitive sports and had exercised to stay in shape, but after so much time spent immobile, the sheer pleasure of moving my body felt liberating, and that summer was when the true athlete in me really started to emerge. I wanted to push my miraculous body further than it had ever gone. I was sure I could actually feel my muscles wrapping themselves around my put-back-together bones, protecting them. I would swim from the dock to a buoy set far out in the lake, then to a second one and back to the dock, until I heard the wake-up call, when I would swim back to the dock and pull myself up, breathless and jelly legged.

Some evenings I would return to the lake after dinner, swimming the triangle again. The harder it got, the more I loved it. Feeling my heart beating, my breath coming faster, knowing that my body had been shattered and now it was whole, mine to love and take care of, made it easier to break through the pain. This was nothing compared to the agony of those first steps I had taken in my driveway, the swimming a joy after having to be still and sore in my hospital bed, day after day. I chose this pain, and it wasn't one I had to fear. And then I would break through and it would become effortless, my strokes long and smooth. I would stay in for so long that when I was done my arms and legs would be noodles, my stomach muscles knots, and my body feeling as though it weighed a thousand pounds without the water to carry it.

Once every summer session there was an organized five-mile early morning swim across the length of the lake, and all summer I practiced for it. It started at three thirty in the morning, and each swimmer had a canoe with two counselors paddling next to them. Mine were Cody and our friend Barclay, who had both, in keeping with Skylake tradition, stayed up drinking and smoking pot all night until they were due down at the docks. When I got down to the lake they were in fine form, with plenty of beer in the bottom of the canoe, for what would turn out to be a four-hour journey. It was still dark, so I tried to vaguely follow the tree line. I kept swimming off course, and my hearing aids were out, so I was unable to hear them as they yelled and laughed, trying to get me back on track. Between my inability to see and hear and their inebriated state we must have added at least a mile to the course, and it's no wonder that I came in dead last. But it was my first major athletic accomplishment, and when I emerged from the water, breathless and beaming, I'm not sure I'd ever felt so proud of myself.

That summer stands out like a dream. I was whole again, with my accident behind me, not aware that a few short months later I would find out, on a cold, snowy day in Michigan, just what was in store for me.

20

When I got to the University of Michigan, one of the first things that I did was to go to the Services for Students with Disabilities office, where I was pointed to the director of Deaf and Hard of Hearing Services. I wasn't sure what to expect and had only a vague idea of how they might be able to help me. What I found there was extraordinary, and who I found even more so. The moment I walked in, the director, Joni Smith, greeted me warmly. She was a jovial woman in her midfifties whose friendly blue eyes and incongruously girly voice immediately put me at ease. She was like gingerbread and warm milk, someone I was instantly comfortable with and felt safe around. She also turned out to be the fiercest advocate I had ever met. Her grandparents had been deaf, and she herself had been a sign language interpreter for Bill and Hillary Clinton, Kofi Annan, the Dalai Lama, and many others.

As accomplished as she was, though, her greatest passion was making sure that her students got the help that they needed and were entitled to. I don't think that I recognized then what a burden I thought that my disabilities were to other people. A part of me was furious that I needed to ask for help from anyone, and another part of me felt ashamed. Which, Joni made very clear that first day, was total bullshit. I had no idea just how many rights I was legally entitled to until she explained it to me, and made it clear that I wasn't a nuisance in asking for help. She taught me crucial lessons in advocating for myself, ones that I would need later, when I would be out in the real world, where there wasn't someone to help me, and where people were not nearly as kind and accommodating as they were here. I think it's difficult for so many of us, especially women, to advocate for ourselves, and Joni's encouragement gave me the strength to do that in all areas of my life.

She also taught me that I should never take no for an answer when it came to getting what I needed. I had wanted to remain anonymous in my classes and would quietly explain this to my professors and ask them to make an announcement in class to see if there was anyone who would agree to take careful notes, and in return be paid for taking them. Most of my professors were great about it, though occasionally I'd get one who didn't understand what I needed or who would say no. Joni was a sweetheart, but when it came to services, she was a force to be reckoned with. If a professor didn't help me, she would call them, and her sweet, girly voice would turn fierce and steely. "This is not an option," she would tell them, "and if this is an issue in the future I will have to bring it to the university's attention."

Joni was also my confidante. The tinnitus had just begun when I started at Michigan, and when I left the doctor's office, not with a prescription for something that would soothe it but with a diagnosis of certain deafness and blindness with an uncertain timeline, she was one of the first people I told. I could cry with Joni, and I could be myself without reservation.

I would walk into her office, feeling terribly about myself, and she would remind me that my disabilities were not my fault, and tell me how beautiful and smart I was, and steer the conversation toward all of the stuff that was right, and not wrong, with me. I watched the sense of fulfillment that she got from helping others and recognized that it was a trait that we shared, and it made me proud to be anything like this wonderful woman, this dynamo. As I got to know her, I found out more about her life, which hadn't been easy. But she didn't focus on the past, she lived in the present, and no matter how busy she was, she would always make time for me. She didn't pity me or see me as my disabilities. I felt like I had found a role model for who, and how, I wanted to be. I was able to accept her help, something that has always been hard for me, because the kind of help that Joni was offering was a kind that taught me to help myself, which made all the difference.

Joni encouraged me to learn sign language. Though the hope was that I would someday in the distant future be a candidate for a cochlear implant, which would allow me to hear, however robotically, that still seemed like a science fiction fantasy, and I knew that signing would help me, even now, to be able to communicate more fully with people. When I learned that Michigan was offering its first-ever course in sign language, Joni immediately made sure that I got a spot in that small class, since it was much in demand. I would learn a language that would come to be invaluable to me.

What humans can accomplish out of necessity is extraordinary. Communication is a need: We are a storytelling people, and we need to tell others our stories. Currently, about seventy million people in the world use sign, allowing them to live as full and rich a life as any hearing person.

Though it was not officially taught until the eighteenth century, mentions of sign language show up as early as the fifth century B.C., when Plato quotes Socrates as saying, "If we hadn't a voice or a tongue, and wanted to express things to one another, wouldn't we try to make signs by moving our hands, head, and the rest of our body, just as dumb people do at present?"

By the late 1700s the first free school for the deaf, in France, had been established by Abbe Charles-Michel de l'Épeé, and the deaf children who came to it all brought the signs they had used to communicate with their families at home. By learning and collating these signs, l'Épée began to construct a complete language, the standard language of sign was soon born, and schools for the deaf spread across Europe.

The American School for the Deaf, the first of its kind in the United States, was founded in 1817 by Thomas Gallaudet and Laurent Clerc, and Gallaudet University, which opened in 1864, was, and remains, the only liberal arts college primarily for the deaf and hard of hearing in the United States and the world.

Sign language is beautiful. It is a robust and exciting language, constantly changing and growing, the way that all modern languages do. It is also the only way to communicate two languages at once, which, if you think about it, is incredibly cool. In addition to hand signs, there is an incredible amount of animation in faces, which is a huge part of the language. You can be tired, or you can be *tired;* it's all about how strongly you gesture and how much your face conveys. Things tend to be more direct, as well, in a way that I find refreshing but that might not fly in the hearing community. Such as: You have gained weight and stop to chat with a deaf friend whom you haven't seen in a while.

After the hellos, your friend points at your stomach and then signs, by blowing out her cheeks and using her hands to mime her own body puffing up, that you have gotten fatter. If a friend said those words to you, it would probably hurt or anger you. But because there is not much language wasted in sign, there is an honesty and a lack of pretense. You're not being judged, it's just a more direct way of communicating. It is still possible, and necessary, to have a deep conversation, a long, involved, philosophical one or a sweet, slow, loving one, but it's time-consuming, and requires a great deal of concentration.

Being part of the deaf community is something that you have to work at. You have to make it very clear that you are willing to put in the time and effort to communicate and make friends with people who are hearing impaired, and integrating myself into the deaf community was not easy to do. It is a group that sets itself apart, quite intentionally, partly because in the deaf community people do not consider their lack of hearing to be a disability and partly because they have often been misunderstood, misrepresented, and ill-treated by much of the hearing world. They were historically treated as though they had inferior intelligence, and many hearing people seem uncomfortable in the company of someone who is deaf. It is natural for people to want to communicate in their own language, and for the deaf, sign language is the only one that they have. For me, it can be such a relief to be with my deaf friends; it is, despite my diminishing vision, a language that I can still communicate more easily in.

It's often just too hard for me to have a casual talk with a stranger, or with anyone, for that matter, who isn't completely engaged; for me, a conversation requires effort and total concentration, and it's amazing, once you notice it, how hard it is for most people to give someone else their full attention. It would be hard for me, too, if it wasn't a requirement at this point, but it's also a lot more rewarding. Looking right at someone, not over their shoulder to see who else is in the room, and really focusing on what they're saying, usually leads to a much more intimate and interesting conversation, if they're willing to do the same.

When you communicate with someone who is deaf, they always give you their full attention; there is no other way to communicate when you are using your hands and eyes as your ears. You have to be fully present.

. . . .

People talk a lot about "living in the moment" and "being present." Of course, I wouldn't wish what I have on anyone, and I would never have chosen it, but it has given me an extraordinary ability to understand profoundly what living in the moment really means and to always try my best to do just that.

I don't mean living each day as if it were my last. I have been there, done that. I've gone bungee jumping and skydiving. There have been times when there were too many guys, too much drinking, a never-ending whirlwind of "let's grab life by the balls." But I've learned that not only is it impossible to keep up that frantic pace, in the end, it's also not very fulfilling. I have what many people would call an enormous (some might say excessive) amount of energy, and staying still is just not in my nature, but never pausing to catch my breath is not the way to appreciate a world that is slowly—and sometimes not so slowly—going silent and dark for me. And while mine is an accelerated decline, one that will leave me with decades of blindness and deafness—many more than I'll spend with hearing and vision, if

I live a long and healthy life—the end is inevitable for all of us. In some ways, I feel lucky to never be able to forget that.

By living in the moment I mean truly appreciating every day, every minute, that I can. I remember to watch the trees in bloom, when the apple and cherry blossoms spend their precious few weeks in spring with us, and even though they're fuzzy now, losing their edges, even though I can only see small pieces of them at a time, I'm so happy to be able to see them at all. I love to watch people's faces. I probably stare too much, but someday I won't see anyone's face, so I look and look, burning the images of the people I love into my brain before they are, for me, forever frozen in time.

Nothing is permanent, and while we all live with this fact, it's an easy one to put aside. To save for another day. We're all dying, but for me, two enormous parts are going at an accelerated rate, and that gives me the ability to remember to notice what I can, while I can. Don't underestimate yourself; you probably would, too. We all have the ability to appreciate and gather every bit of joy that we can from this world. We just forget to.

I appreciate what I have, because I have less today than I had yesterday, and more than I will tomorrow. I am no Pollyanna, though I am an optimist, which, in my case, is an extraordinary stroke of luck. There have been, of course, times when I've been as furious and frustrated and heartbroken as you can imagine I would be. I have been through times of profound sadness for the losses I have experienced, and for those yet to come. Times when I have woken up in the middle of the night, when I finally have the time and space for it, and let the sadness wash over me. I had been told for so long that I would go blind and deaf, and now I'm actually, really experiencing it. Even now, I'm not sure where I am.

When I'll cross over. I used to think of my thirties as so old, and now I feel so young. I lie awake in the dark, in the complete silence. I don't know how quiet it is, really, if the garbage trucks have already started their noisy routes, if a dog is barking outside or a drunk crowd is laughing their way down the block. I can't hear anything, except what's in my own head. Sometimes I can't help but wonder how it will be at the very end, though I try not to. Will I have a last clear image that I see, before my pinprick of a hole finally closes up forever? Or will things just blur more and more, an impressionist painting that gets increasingly less recognizable until finally it's just a swirl of fading color, and then nothing? Will the last authentic sound I hear be a laugh, a cry, a subway rumbling into the station?

This is not a productive line of thought, but allowing myself to really feel these emotions has been a crucial part of how I cope with the reality of my condition. When I am overcome with it, I often cry and even beg whomever or whatever is out there to just let me be, to let me hold on to what I have left. *Please.* And then I move on. I don't feel like the cards I've been dealt are unfair, I don't think that life is that complicated, and I know that pity is a trap that will deplete my self-esteem and take away time that I don't have to waste. I choose instead to be grateful: to be happy with what I have today, and to be optimistic about tomorrow. It's a conscious choice, and one that takes effort, but what's the alternative? What other choice do any of us have if we want to live our lives to the fullest?

If we knew everything that we'd eventually have to face in life, it would paralyze most of us. I have to prepare myself, as much as I can, for the inevitable. Because if I spent all of my time focusing on that future place devoid of light and sound, I would have missed, would be missing, so much in the present.

When I hear people say how fragile life is, how it can all be taken away from us in a second, I always think that, for me, it's not life that feels fragile, it's the living of it, in this precarious place between seeing and blindness, and hearing and deafness. I used to experience glimpses of what it felt like to be blind or deaf throughout the day, reminding me of how different my life is from others'. Today, I teeter along a fine line between the two, and which side of it I'm on seems to differ from day to day, and sometimes even hour to hour. Some days are better than others, and while there may be fluctuations, things are, as they say, only trending in one direction. This is what's happening. The line is going to blur until I can't see it anymore.

21

A year after my diagnosis, when I was twenty, I went home for winter break. Though Cody and I hadn't seen each other in a while, we always hooked up when we saw each other. This time, though, when I went home, he was distant and seemed to have no interest in anything romantic.

At the time, I didn't know that he had a new girlfriend; I think that he was apprehensive about telling me and hurting my feelings. I was sure that he was no longer attracted to me and that if I just looked better, he would want me again. At the time, I didn't recognize that what happened next was not really about Cody at all.

While I had never been overweight, I became convinced that I needed to be thin to be happy. When I got back to school I immediately joined Weight Watchers and started going to the gym daily, losing a pound a week, just the way they tell you to. As I started to see the results, though, instead of sticking with the program, I wanted to push myself further, work harder, get as thin as I could. So I started to exercise more, sometimes as much as three hours in the morning before my classes, or for hours at night if I couldn't fit that in. Not the fun kind of going to the gym, chatting with friends on the StairMaster, happily listening to music as I climbed, but serious exercise, all I could get. I'm well aware that this is not an original affliction for young women, but I made the same mistake so many others have. I believed that if I kept it together and looked perfect, maybe no one would notice the things that were wrong with me, all of my flaws.

I think many people, particularly young women, are familiar with this feeling. On top of trying to keep it all together with studying, socializing, exercising, and trying to be liked by everyone around me, I was keeping secrets from most people. I didn't want to talk about my eyes and ears, and I struggled not to let my limp—and my continuing pain—show. The idea of people feeling sorry for me made me physically sick, so instead of focusing on my disabilities, which were totally out of my control, I focused on the things that I could control: eating and exercising, and keeping myself as fit and attractive as I could.

The Rebecca I wanted people to know was fun-loving, easygoing, hardworking. She loved to dance and to flirt. She was a good friend, someone who made things more fun. I wanted boys to think that I was pretty and baggage free, but I was struggling so hard to like myself. It wasn't my fault that I had Usher syndrome. Intellectually I understood that. Why though, deep down, did I still sometimes think, as I had since my first diagnosis, that it confirmed some fundamental wrongness in me? I was worried that if people knew I had Usher syndrome they would think of me as less fun, and that I would eventually become a chore and that they might be nice just because they felt sorry for me. I knew, too, that I wouldn't be able to hide it forever. So I wanted to be wonderful now. I loved it when guys looked at me, their eyes telling me how much they liked what they saw. I wanted to keep that feeling as long as I could.

Why is it that we sometimes have to learn the same lessons over and over? After my accident I came to appreciate my body for its resilience and power. I exercised to feel the joy of all my working parts, to make myself strong. Now I had started to take it for granted again, that I had a working, healthy body. Now I wanted to make it perfect, even though I knew deep down that it never could be.

I had a dream one night that I'll never forget, one so clear that it wouldn't take an analyst to understand the meaning of it. It was during the height of my eating and exercise disorder, where I would work out for hours a day and then binge, often on peanut butter, late at night, when my body, having starved all day, was desperate for the high-fat calories and nutrients it provided.

In the dream, my hearing aids were covered in peanut butter. I kept wiping, digging into every crevice, trying desperately to get them clean, but no matter how hard I tried, no matter how much I cleaned off, there was still more. I just couldn't get all of it out.

That summer, when I went home, I was thin, fit, and perfectly toned. It was all that I thought about. I took diet pills—those terrible ones full of ephedrine that are now banned—and subsisted on as little food as I could. Breakfast was a thinly sliced apple that I would dip into a low-calorie, artificially sweetened yogurt. Lunch was usually carrots dipped in salsa, and dinner would be a large salad full of vegetables, skinless chicken breast, and fat-free dressing.

Cody and I ran into each other early that summer, at the gym. He thought that I looked fantastic, and we made plans to get together right away. He had broken up with his girlfriend, the one whom I didn't know about until years later, and I was sure that his renewed interest was all about how great I now looked. Even though this was Cody, who had loved me long before any of this, I was convinced that it was all about my body. It was just the reinforcement that I was looking for but was, of course, the worst thing for me.

I would spend the next several years struggling to like and accept my body, wasting so much time and energy, the way so many women do, judging myself by my reflection in the mirror.

22

That same summer, as I painstakingly counted every calorie and exercised fanatically, I started to look into services available to people living with disabilities in California. Joni had encouraged me to do it, and at first I dragged my feet about it, until my mother's nudging and my own curiosity got the better of me. I hated thinking of myself that way, as someone who needed help. Like people for whom parking spaces were reserved, or someone on the bus whom others would jump up and give their seat to. While I admired others for their bravery, and for being able to advocate for what they needed, I still couldn't imagine myself as part of that. So even though I called, I told myself that my decision to learn Braille had more to do with the fact that I thought it would be cool and interesting to learn, like people learn Italian, rather than something that would become a necessity for me down the road.

Braille had always fascinated me, ever since I was a girl reading the *Little House* books, in which Laura's sister Mary goes blind from encephalitis. Laura's family sacrificed and worked so that Mary could attend the Iowa College for the Blind, where she studied all of her subjects in Braille. It was an immeasurable gift from a poor family to their daughter, but one they deemed important above all else, for her to be educated. I remembered the illustration of beautiful Mary, a serene smile on her face as she returned from school, and my imagination ran wild with the idea of being able to read through the touch of my fingertips. So much so that I would often close my eyes while gliding my hands across the page just to pretend that I, too, could read Braille.

I got a call from Ruth, a woman with the California Department of Rehabilitation, who was calling to set up an appointment to come to my house for my first Braille lesson. While I had never seen her, I was sure, as soon as I heard her voice, that she was blind. Her speech felt too exuberant, somehow socially awkward, and almost cartoonish. I hated that this was the first thing that came to mind when speaking to Ruth on the phone, and that I didn't feel—or sound—as enthusiastic about meeting her and learning Braille as she seemed to be about teaching me, that I was already recoiling from this kind-sounding, cheerful woman. As she chatted on, telling me what the lesson would entail and arranging a time for us, my mind wandered, her Disneylike voice bringing me into a dreamlike state, where I imagined the two of us standing at the gates of a children's theme park. I pictured her in pigtails with large red bows, handing me a great big rainbow-colored lollipop, opening the gates, and singsonging, "Hello, Rebecca! Welcome to Blind Land. Just take my hand and I'll show you the way!"

I shuddered and came back to the sound of Ruth's voice, knowing that there was no way I was going to walk through those gates, imaginary or otherwise. I spoke to her with as much kindness and compassion as I could muster, despising myself but unable to shake the feeling that I was somehow the one doing her the favor. I deceived myself into believing that I was doing some kind of charity work, helping this blind woman feel good about herself, giving her a job. That she was blind, and I was just pretending to be.

At that time, I hadn't yet understood what going blind really meant. I couldn't really recognize how much vision loss I had experienced since my original diagnosis at twelve and still didn't totally equate that loss with going blind, as crazy as that sounds. I had always interpreted the message that I was going blind as referring to something that was going to happen to me when I grew up, which I certainly hadn't, and I tried for as little self-reflection as possible on this subject. I still separated my actual self from my diagnosis, too, becoming comfortably detached whenever I had to explain it and how it affected me to people who would ask.

I met Ruth at the top of our driveway to help her maneuver her way to our house. It was hard enough to find the narrow, snaking path that hid along the side of our neighbors' driveway; for someone who was blind it would have been close to impossible. As Ruth carefully stepped out of the Access-A-Ride van, I greeted her and extended my upper arm toward her, bending it at the elbow for her to hold on to so that I could guide her. I prided myself on doing this expertly. I'd attended enough Foundation Fighting Blindness conferences and events to know the best way to guide a blind person while walking, and I could sympathize with her condition. Empathy, however, was still far beyond my reach.

Ruth had been blind since birth. Her eyes were a cloudy color somewhere between white and light blue, and they couldn't focus. Her left eye veered up and to the right while her right eye seemed to be looking directly toward the sky. It was clear to me that she had never been sighted, and I found myself fascinated by her now that she was in front of me. It was amazing to watch the ways in which she had adapted to a sighted world: the way she spoke and listened, and the way she seemed to trust me absolutely as her guide. The trust seemed to lend her an almost childlike quality, and it made me a little uncomfortable, and even angry for her, that she was forced to trust me to lead her responsibly. It seemed so incredibly unfair and I didn't know where to direct that frustration, except by making sure that I did my very best to make her feel safe and accommodated.

I gave Ruth my arm to hold so that she could feel the movement of my body by the way my arm moved, and let her know when there were stairs or exactly what was coming directly ahead of us so that she would not be caught off guard. When we reached the steep stairwell, I told her that there was a railing on her left side that she could hold on to; I counted each step down and gave her forewarning when our last step was approaching. I loved doing this, helping her and feeling needed. I've always felt so fulfilled by offering small gestures of help and seeing others do it, and I felt ease and comfort in helping her, which helped distract me from the real reason Ruth was coming to my house that day. After all, I was still the one helping her here.

My parents had a large, easily excitable Bernese mountain dog named Tally who would bark enthusiastically and hurl her gigantic body at visitors when they arrived. As Ruth and I slowly walked down the second steep flight of stairs into the house, Tally began to bark and dance in circles to welcome us. Ruth laughed, understanding right away that Tally was simply a noisemaker with no interest in harming anyone. Maybe it was because of her acute hearing, extra sensitive because of her blindness, and her ability to hear the nuances of sound that most people miss, that she was able to instantly understand Tally's bark. It occurred to me then that maybe she had also heard the reticence in my voice, and possibly too the disdain that I didn't understand or want to feel and knew I didn't have any right to.

As we reached the door, Tally approached us and I quickly tried to shoo her away so that Ruth's path wouldn't be obstructed. But when Ruth felt the brush of Tally's tail against her leg she stopped walking and slowly leaned down with her hand extended for Tally to smell. As Tally happily explored her hand, Ruth spoke to her sweetly: "Hello, pretty girl. It's very nice to meet you." I thought to myself how ironic it was that Ruth called Tally a "pretty girl," even though she couldn't see her and couldn't possibly know what a dog looked like. What I thought then was that it was just a response that she had learned through hearing it repetitively from others, rather than by personal experience. Now that I'm much closer to where Ruth was, I wonder. What does "pretty" mean when you can't see? My dog Olive is the most adorable thing in the world to me, but it's not just her puppy eyes, her lithe, curly-haired body and proud golden tail. It's her warmth, enthusiasm, and curiosity, her simple doggie radiance. Maybe that's what "pretty" meant to Ruth. I wish I'd asked her.

Once we got ourselves settled it became abundantly clear that any thoughts I had had about this being for her benefit were woefully misguided. I was amazed by how effortlessly Ruth's hands flew over the bumpy white page as she read the Braille directions to me. I watched her face, feeling almost voyeuristic because she couldn't look back at me. I wondered if she could feel me staring at her. I was so curious about her expressions, her rate of speech, and how keenly alert she seemed. I kept having to remind myself to stop staring rudely and would look back down at the page she was reading, almost as spellbound by her hands as I was by her face.

When it was my turn to put my hands on the Braille I realized how desensitized my fingers were and how difficult it was to feel the difference between each letter. I have always thought of myself as very tactile, my sense of touch heightened to help compensate for my declining eyes and ears. But after putting my hands on the paper filled with hundreds of words coded by little white bumps, I was humbled. I thought of Helen Keller, who had never read a word or heard one in her living memory, and I felt like an idiot for not realizing what hard work this was going to be.

When my first lesson in Braille was through, I promised Ruth that I would practice, even though I had a sneaking suspicion that I wouldn't; after all, I didn't need to—I could still see. I walked her to the top of both steep stairways and up the cobbled brick driveway to the sidewalk, where she was to be picked up by the Access-A-Ride bus service. Ruth told me that she had let the bus driver know where and when she needed to be picked up, and since I had a doctor's appointment that I needed to drive myself to, I thanked her and rather unceremoniously left her there.

When I drove out of the driveway a few minutes later I saw her waiting patiently for the bus to pick her up, and I raised my hand instinctively to wave good-bye, then quickly lowered it as I realized that it was a futile gesture. About an hour later, as I drove home from my appointment and got close to my house, I realized that Ruth was still standing there in the bright sun, waiting.

It wasn't that I didn't know what I should do—me, to whom helping others had always come so easily. But I drove right by her, knowing that I was behaving horribly, that I was selfish and un-grateful and committing a huge betrayal, to her and to myself, but unable to help it. I stared at her as I passed, overwhelmed by guilt and sadness. I felt as though I had taken advantage of her—like I was given a glimpse into her life and what it meant to be blind and I'd rejected her and said, "No thanks, this is not for me." At that time I couldn't even admire her for who she was or her independence, because I was so horribly afraid of what she represented: my future.

Sometimes, when I think about the past, there are years that seem to have passed by in mere moments. Those few hours with Ruth, though, seem to have slowed down in my memory, every detail seared into me. I'd give almost anything to go back to that day. To stop and gently take her arm, lead her to my car, and drive her home. To thank her genuinely and ask her the questions that I had been so afraid of at the time. But I didn't. I never even called her again.

After Ruth I vowed that I would never, ever let myself behave that way again. That had never been who I was; I had always, al-ways been the one to help and to volunteer, to lend a hand to someone who needed it.

I had let Ruth down, and I had let myself down. I had come face-to-face with the thing that scared me most in the world, and I had run away, and I was so ashamed of myself. No matter how much good I had tried to do, or how many people I had worked to help, I felt like I had undone it in an instant. Though I didn't know it at the time, that day fundamentally changed me.

I never told anyone about it; I was too ashamed. I didn't learn any Braille that day, either, nor have I really since—though it's high on the list of *things I absolutely must know and do before I am totally blind that I really need to make time for.* However, I learned so many other lessons that day, ones that will stay with me forever.

. . . .

One of the hardest things for me to accept is how much I now need people's help, and that I always will, increasingly so as life goes on. Countless people have risen to the task—from a stranger who offers his or her arm to help me across the street to the advocates for the blind and deaf who have taught me to ask for what I need. From my best friends, Caroline and Alan, who can sign and tactile-sign with me, to Peter, who never lets a joke go by without repeating it to make sure that I hear it, to my parents, who have done everything to find ways to help me, to teach me how to help myself, and immersed themselves in the research community. They have all given so much to me, and I need to remember to be grateful for that, to accept that help as the gift that it is and not run up against the walls of my frustration for needing it.

When a friend who is blind can't find the coffee sitting on the table in front of her, it feels very natural for me to lead her hand to it. Even when Caroline helps me in the same way I have to try not to flinch: My reaction is to pull my hand away or to say, "I've got it, thanks," uncomfortable and insecure about my need for help. I've found, though, that people want to do this; the urge to help others is a basic part of human nature. Not only shouldn't I deny the people who love me that, I can't. I need them. I try to remember that they need me, too. Even though I'm the one with the disability, it's not a one-way street.

23

I walked uneasily down the prison corridor, my shoes echoing loudly on the floor, my folder full of painstakingly made pamphlets tucked under my arm. I had already been searched and patted down, and now I was getting catcalls from a group of male prisoners being led down the hallway past me. They raised their shackled hands together to the side of their head, making the universal sign for a telephone, and as soon as I walked by they said, "Call me, baby. I'm in cell four seven one two . . ." My cheeks flushed and I looked down, but before I could get too nervous, or even feel the most tiny bit flattered, I heard them saying the same things to the broad-shouldered, stern-faced, middle-aged female guard walking several feet behind me, as they would to any female who got within calling distance of them.

I was a senior at Michigan and taking a small upperclassmen seminar called "Women in Prison." In addition to the academic work, we were required to participate in some way with the inmates or families directly. Some people spent the semester planning the Christmas party for the children and family members of the women who were imprisoned. Others opted to work with some of the children of the incarcerated in an after-school program. What I wanted to do was to work with the inmates themselves. Reading all of the research and studies about these women felt like such a secondhand approach to actually getting to know them, which was what I knew I needed to do if I was going to have a better understanding of what their lives were really like, both behind bars and out on the street.

I knew I wouldn't be given access to the prison just to sit around and chat with these women or because I was really interested in getting to know them. So I developed a "health class" to teach at the prison, which would include information about safer sex practices, sexually transmitted diseases, rights for prisoners to medical care, mental health support, and nutrition. I would go into the prison to teach two days a week.

The large cell block where I would be teaching held about twenty women, though I never saw all of them at once. There was a sleeping area with bunk beds at the very back that was kept dark, and, given my vision and where I was, I didn't think it would be a good idea for me to wander back there and see if anyone else felt like joining the class. I was given a quick, bored introduction by the guard and then sat down in the main room, a very brightly lit open space with a TV, two tables, and a scattering of chairs. The TV was on, as it always was, and I was competing with Jerry Springer as I began talking to the women. He definitely had the edge. At first, most of the women took little to no interest in my visit. They looked me up and down skeptically and asked a lot of questions, and then, unimpressed with my attempts at professional-sounding answers, their eyes flicked back to Jerry and his parade of outrageous guests. I couldn't blame them. The lesson plans I had created and printed out for them initially remained in neat stacks in the center of both of the tables. These women didn't care about going over any more paperwork, and their experience with people coming in and trying to "help" them probably had never come to much good.

After the first couple of visits, I started to realize that the only time they really focused on me was when I completely focused on them. Not as statistics or students, but as people. When I asked them real, specific questions about their lives and their families. What they really wanted, like most of us, was just to be heard. So instead of teaching, I'd sit down with several women around a table and listen to them talk, and I'd leave each week's pamphlets on the table for them to look over on their own.

They'd share their stories about what was happening in their lives before they were incarcerated, how they afforded to live—many through prostitution or selling drugs, or being the middleman for a boyfriend who was selling them. Many of them shared stories about how they had risked their lives and freedom to protect their boyfriends or husbands from getting caught. There were women of all ages—from eighteen to seventy-three—and most of them had children, some grandchildren as well. Some of the kids were already in the foster care system, others had relatives to take care of them. When they talked about their kids I could hear pride in their voices, but also guilt and sadness. Some would meet my eyes but others would look away, telling me that they wanted better lives for their children than they had had, but they seemed to feel helpless in trying to accomplish that. None of them were in prison for the first time.

It occurred to me then, as it so often has since, how crucial the impact of childhood and family is for all of us. Just about every one of these women had the deck stacked against her from the beginning—being born to a teenage mother, into poverty, or into an abusive family; growing up in a dangerous neighborhood; and often, all of the above. Listening to their stories woke me up during a time in my life when I felt too self-absorbed and wrapped up in my own issues, and altered my perspective on my own life in a lasting way.

Yes, it sucked that I was going blind and deaf. But that's what I was born with, part of what my deck had been stacked with. I was also born into a loving, generous, wacky and wonderful family. A family with its problems and heartbreaks, like all families, but a never-endingly adoring one. I could sit there and call myself lucky.

By the time my carefully devised course came to an end, one thing was very clear—these women were not interested in learning whatever it was I'd come to teach them, and I had been naive to think that they would be. Most of them didn't even know that I was there to teach them anything, but they were so desperate to talk and really be listened to that I never felt like I was wasting anybody's time. In fact, I loved it.

It was one of the really clarifying times in my life where I realized that *listening* to other people was a gift that I had, something that I was really good at. Ironic, considering how hard it can be for me to hear, but perhaps not so surprising. Maybe it was the fact that I had to work harder at it that made it so important to me to really be able to hear people. Focusing and giving something my undivided attention in order to be able to really communicate was a necessity for me, and it was a skill that I had honed. In listening I had found a way to help these women, and to help myself.

I went there with the hope of having an impact on the prisoners' lives and educating them. I left unsure of whether I'd had any real effect on them at all, but they had an enormous, and lasting, impact on me. I realized that this was the work that I wanted to do. I wanted to listen to people's stories, and, ultimately, to help them figure out how to rise up from their difficulties and how to recognize and change patterns that weren't working in their lives. Most of all, though, I wanted to be there to listen to what people needed to say.

After that I volunteered for a shelter for battered women and children. This became the ongoing theme in my life: The more I put myself out there, helping other people, and the less time I spent thinking about myself—my disabilities, my weight, whatever else I thought was wrong with me—the better I felt.

24

There have been times when I have stopped and thought about how unlikely it is to be born with Usher syndrome. Just the odds. So minuscule. So, when the winds of fate (and my amazing mother) brought together something that seemed almost as unlikely, but wonderful, it felt miraculous.

Since the moment that my mother learned of my diagnosis of RP, she has done everything in her power to connect me to the right resources and the support I have needed, and she has helped me prepare, emotionally and otherwise, for what lies ahead. She is an incredible force of nature.

After I was first diagnosed my mom began working as a volunteer for the Foundation Fighting Blindness, eventually leaving her job to work full-time for the organization as their western regional executive director, tirelessly raising funds for research, but well aware that, because my disorder was so rare, it was unlikely that it would be a top priority for researchers. We had no way of knowing then that on the other side of the globe an effort was already under way to identify the genetic mutation causing

Usher syndrome type III, nor could we have imagined that our family would end up playing a key role in this process.

Working for the Foundation, my mom had access to some of the country's best doctors, several of whom were doing some of the most cutting-edge eye research out there. FFB was funding research at the School of Optometry at UC Berkeley, and my mother wanted to meet with the doctor spearheading the effort, Dr. John Flannery. When she did, in the fall of 2000, it happened that he had just returned from a trip to Finland, where, it turned out, he had been invited to meet with an ophthalmologist/geneticist at Helsinki University about collaborating on research that she was doing on Usher syndrome type III. Apparently, an enclave of affected individuals had been living for decades in a small town in southern Finland, and the Finnish government was funding some of that country's top vision and hearing researchers, who had been working to clone and characterize the Usher III gene. The goal was to find the offending mutation in the transport of the gene's protein within the cell so that a treatment for Usher III could be developed.

My mom was stunned to learn that targeted research on a disorder as rare as mine was already under way, and even more astonished that it was happening in her own backyard, with Dr. Flannery doing work on the disorder at UC Berkeley. Until then, we had always been told that nobody knew for sure if there actually was a separate Usher III gene. Dr. Flannery was equally amazed when my mom told him that doctors believed that I was likely affected with Usher III. He confided that, despite all of their work to date, the Finnish scientific team was finding it particularly complicated to characterize this particular gene.

Always proactive, my mother asked whether the research in

Finland might benefit from receiving DNA samples from our family, though we were Ashkenazi Jews, not of Finnish descent. Was there any way that our DNA might be able to help the researchers "crack the code"? Dr. Flannery put my mother in touch with the lead Finnish researcher, Dr. Eeva-Marja Sankila, at Helsinki University.

Dr. Sankila was thrilled to hear from an affected American family and welcomed our participation in her research. She promptly sent blood-draw kits to the three generations of my immediate relatives—my grandparents, parents, and brothers. At the time, we were spread out across the United States, and Daniel was studying in France, but everyone immediately drew their samples and sent them back in, fingers crossed. What followed for my mother were many months of watchful waiting. For me, it still seemed so distant and remote, light-years away from anything that could ever possibly help me, that I put it out of my mind, focusing on graduating from college and trying to figure out what to do next.

My mother got the chance, a few months later, to meet with Dr. Sankila, a brilliant woman who exuberantly told her about the work she was doing. She explained that while her team had cloned the gene and isolated the Finnish mutation, it did not match ours, though in her tracing of our family's DNA, she had discovered that it would be through my father's mother and my mother's father that I had inherited the disorder. A small part of the gene had yet to be decoded, and Dr. Sankila and her team were still looking for possible additional mutations. She had just met with an Israeli researcher who had access to additional DNA samples from Ashkenazi Jews in Israel. She was eager to provide Dr. Sankila's team with more samples in the hope that this would help the team discover the Ashkenazi mutation.

I got the call from my mother in December of 2002. I could tell as soon as I answered the phone that she had been crying, but before I had the chance to worry, the words flew out of her mouth. "They found you! The Finnish researchers found the genetic mutation that's causing your Usher III!"

I matched her enthusiasm immediately, jumping out of my chair and yelling, "They did?!" Then I stood there for a moment, stunned, and finally asked, "What does that mean?" My mother understood so much more than I did about the science of what was happening to me. While I dealt with the day-to-day challenges, she was actually focusing on the bigger picture, something I had yet to really grasp.

"It means that they now know what they are dealing with and can begin to figure out a way to stop it," she explained, and I could hear the love and happiness in her voice. My mother had spent the last ten years working toward this, struggling to find out anything and everything she could, and she knew that any treatment or cure relied on this critical information. Now, finally, someone could take the first steps toward looking for a treatment. This was actually a real, tangible step, something that could give us at least a glimmer of hope. A first step, but a huge one.

"Oh, Mom!" I cried, and I held the phone against my ear and wept. She did the same, and I felt so close to her, and so proud of her, and so, so lucky to have a mother who loved me this much.

"There are going to be many more bright days ahead for you," she told me.

"Do you really think so?" I asked. I spent so much time trying not to get my hopes up and just focusing on what I had to tackle in the present, but at this moment, I let myself hope, just a little. And her answer was, "Yes, I'm sure of it!"

And she was right. There isn't a cure yet, though there are glimmers on the horizon. My days are filled with obstacles, but so many of them are also bright, because I have people in my life, like my mother, who are always there for me and help to keep me filled with hope for the future.

25

After college Daniel and I moved to Santa Monica and shared an apartment with our friend Jason. Dan had started law school, striding ahead of me as usual, at the top of his class, while I was answering phones at an international photography syndication agency in the heart of LA, a ridiculous job for someone with limited hearing and a terrible one for someone with body issues. People with all kinds of accents and long, complicated names I usually didn't catch would call, and I was constantly asking them to repeat themselves, still not getting it right, so that when I had to connect them with the person they'd called for, it generally went something like this:

Me: Cherie, there's a woman on the line for you from *Vogue España.*

Cherie: Did you ask her name?

Me: Yep, twice.

Cherie: (sigh) Fine, put it through.

Me: Sorry, Cherie, I'll try harder next time.

As though that would help.

I have no idea why they kept me on; though I was overqualified, even I wouldn't have hired me.

The people calling wanted photos of celebrities and models for their magazines, and before sending them off, our editing department would digitally manipulate the pictures, erasing any blemishes or body imperfections and making the already beautiful women flawless. Though of course I already knew that pictures in magazines had been airbrushed and Photoshopped, I had never before watched the "before and after" process. It was shocking to see that the most famous and gorgeous women on earth actually had imperfections like the rest of us—funky tan lines, bad acne, and cellulite—all of which would be turned into glowing skin and the sleekest of figures. Instead of feeling comforted by this—stars are just like us!—I was reminded every day that being anything less than perfect was unacceptable, and I was so very far from perfect. I was still struggling with my eating disorder and my issues with body image. Of course, the real imperfections, the things about me that could not be fixed, were the ones that I tried not to think about.

It made me angry, though, working in this ridiculous perfection factory. I wanted to rebel, to say "fuck you" and eat whatever I wanted. Of course, I also wanted to be thin and perfect.

The answer, I knew, was to get out of there. Out of the job and out of LA. So I spent much of my time at work researching graduate schools. I spent hours looking online for the types of jobs I was interested in. I had known for a long time now that I wanted to be in a helping profession. I really loved the idea of working in a developing community overseas, but, given my disabilities, I knew that probably wouldn't be a wise decision.

In the meantime I kept answering phones and trying to sneak out of work early so I could drive home while it was still light out. I was never supposed to drive at night, but sometimes I did it anyway, because it was the only way to get anywhere, and I had convinced myself that it was okay. I found out too late that it wasn't remotely okay.

I was driving home one evening, long past dark, on Wilshire Boulevard. I saw the barest flash of a figure before there was a dull thud, and my heart stopped. I was dialing 911 even as I jumped out of my car, swallowing down vomit as I saw the man sitting propped against the front of my car, right where I had hit him. People rushed over, appearing in front of me suddenly, because, of course, I had lost much of my peripheral vision, and it was especially bad at night. Which is why I hadn't seen this man, and why I had absolutely no right to be behind the wheel.

Someone bent down to help him and he got unsteadily to his feet. I started to sob, babbling apologies, and was quickly and quietly assured by an onlooker that the man was drunk. He and his wife had seen the whole thing, and the man had stumbled out from between two parked cars, right in front of my car. It wasn't my fault, they assured me, but I knew better. I hadn't seen him because I had a huge blind spot, and if I had been driving faster I could have killed him. He could have been sober, or a child, or anyone, and I still wouldn't have been able to stop in time; my eyes gave me too little warning. Though the EMTs assured me that he was basically uninjured, and extremely drunk, the scene replayed itself again and again in my head over the next few months, and I felt like I was choking every time I thought about it, knowing how it could have turned out.

. . . .

There are times when I have sensed a sharp acceleration in my hearing or vision loss, usually one or the other. This time—between the driving and my clear inability to hear what I was doing at my job—I felt both, and it made me want to move faster and work harder at the things that I really wanted, quick, before it was too late, before there were more things that I couldn't do. I knew a lot of people who were bumming around after college, feeling aimless, working shitty jobs, and feeling like they had all the time in the world to figure out what it was they wanted. That wasn't who I wanted to be, and I knew very well that I didn't have all the time in the world. One thing I could always hear clearly was the clock ticking.

I had never been one to simply accept feeling miserable, and I hated feeling like I was doing nothing to better my own life or anybody else's. All the jobs that interested me required a master's in either social work or public health. So I started studying for the GRE and applying to graduate schools, setting my sights on Columbia, hoping that New York would give me the independence that I craved and the life that I was ready to begin. I pored over the tiny font in the study guides, squinting to see things in focus until the throbbing behind my eyes became so intense that I had to take a break.

I knew that I also had to do something to make the next several months fun, something that wasn't just studying and working at a dull job that I was terrible at and then waiting to hear back from schools. So I started training for the AIDS/LifeCycle ride, a weeklong, six-hundred-mile ride from San Francisco to LA, knowing that a physical challenge was something that I could rise to, something that would make me feel proud and strong, and just as able-bodied as everybody else. I hoped, too, that it would help me vanquish the monster inside me who obsessed constantly about food. I had been attending Overeaters Anonymous meetings, but, though I knew it was important to talk about my feelings, what I really wanted was to *do* something, to kick my ass into high gear and feel good about myself again.

I finally started to feel normal again, knowing that I was working to move forward in my professional life, push my body hard, and do something that would help others. I was beginning to feel less stuck. I bought a bike and had six months to train and raise money. I couldn't wait. The only thing that gave me pause was that I had never ridden a bike more than a few miles at a time before. Most of my time on two wheels had been spent riding around my neighborhood with my friends, my training wheels remaining on long after everyone else had taken theirs off. A bike was a bike, though, so I figured I'd be fine.

I joined a group of other people who were training, and we would head up into the hills together. At first it was complete, utter torture. But I threw myself into it, the pain in my legs burning every other thought out of my mind. I would fall asleep the instant my head hit the pillow at night, and in the morning when I got out of bed I would walk widely, as though I'd just dismounted a horse, feeling every muscle below my waist, sure that I couldn't possibly handle another day. I quickly grew to love it, though, falling again into what felt like a Stockholm syndrome with the intense, wonderful pain of pushing my body to its limits. It was just the two of us, my bike and me, and I knew, just as I had at Skylake, that I could work through the pain. Was it dangerous for a girl with little eyesight or hearing to be biking over steep, bumpy hills? Probably, but the exhilaration more than made up for it. I couldn't be scared to do things that were a little harder—maybe more than a little—because I couldn't see or hear as well. This was the best that my eyes were ever going to be, and someday I wouldn't be able to bike alone at all. I was going to do it now. I think that in so many ways it was my accident that made me brave. I had fallen as far as you could fall, and I had risen back up again. It made me adaptable and determined, and that has stood me in good stead since.

Three months into my training, I found out that I'd been accepted to Columbia, my first choice, as well as several other schools. UCLA had offered me a free ride, and several people encouraged me to take it, because it would keep me closer to home, and I would be left without the burden of student loans. I thought back on the accident, though, and the terrible sound of my car hitting that man, and knew that there was no way I could stay in LA. Polly encouraged me to take the leap and choose Columbia. She knew that I craved independence and felt trapped by my disabilities in LA. It was scary, the idea of taking on that much debt and living so far from my family, but she intuitively understood that this was what would be best for me, and that the freedom and adventure I wanted lay elsewhere, and helped give me the courage to make my choice. I would be sad to leave Daniel and my family behind but was overjoyed at the idea of stepping out on my own. There had already been so many roadblocks and stops and starts in my life, and I knew there would be many more challenges along the way, but I felt as though I was finally setting off down the path that would be best for me. I was only twenty-four years old, but I knew that I didn't have any time to waste.

Thrilled that what felt like my "real life" was finally going to begin, I threw myself into training for the ride, feeling more motivated than ever. I joyfully quit my job two weeks before the ride, and, as I arrived at the start with thousands of other bikers, I felt a sense of camaraderie and excitement, and I couldn't wait to begin my journey.

As we started biking, I felt anxious and excited but confident I could handle it. It would end up being one of the most physically challenging days of my life. Our training group had built up to twenty-mile rides, and then forty, with the longest being fifty-five. On the first day of the ride, the longest, we doubled that, riding one hundred and ten endless, often agonizing, miles.

The things that saved me were the rest stops that were set up for the riders every thirty miles, each one with its own special theme. One stop had a spa theme, with the "roadies" wearing bathrobes, towels twisted on top of their heads, spa slippers, and facial masks. For another stop we rode around and down a steep hill until we hit a huge sign that said CIRQUE DU SO-GAY followed by roadies dressed up as clowns and circus entertainers. There was no better relief from a long stretch of riding than comedy, eating snacks so good that I probably gained weight, and most importantly, butt butter. Each pit stop had "medic tables" where riders could get all types of first aid care—and on each table sat rows upon rows of paper towels with a dollop of thick ointment. The real name of it was chamois butter, but on the road, it went by the appropriate name of "butt butter," and there was nothing we riders looked forward to more than lubing up with it whenever we could. Not only because it was soothing on our incredibly sore backsides, but because of the comedic factor of having to stand in broad daylight with absolutely no privacy, taking the glop of butt butter in one hand, pulling your riding shorts open at the waist, and applying the creamy substance directly between your legs, getting your hand as far back as you could go in order to lubricate your entire undercarriage. We would all glance over at each other and burst out laughing at how ridiculous we looked. No one cared, though, because it felt so damn good and soothing. We were all riding hard to help fight a plague that had taken so many precious lives, and it just felt so wonderful to stand there and laugh together.

Each night we rode into our campsite, where we bathed in port-a-showers and pitched our own tents to sleep in. There was usually some form of entertainment or a talent show, but the only thing I could think of after dinner was going directly back to my tent to pass out. My tent-mate was another rider named Tiffany who was a few years older than me, who'd originally gotten involved because at twenty-six she was already acting as a foster parent to children living with HIV who needed to be placed in permanent homes. Tiffany and I started out the ride together, but it was soon clear that I was just a speck of dust in her tailwind. Lucky for me, our tent was usually pitched by the time I made my way into the campgrounds in the evenings because she had arrived long before I had. I would have loved to ask her more about her life, but we were both sound asleep the minute we crawled into our sleeping bags.

On the ride, everyone who was HIV positive had a fluorescent orange flag on his or her bike, to let the medics know, so that they could keep a special eye on them. It was so inspiring when someone would pass me with one, and I thought maybe I understood a little of how they felt, triumphant to be able to do what they could with their bodies, willing to push themselves hard, because there is something about knowing that you have limitations that makes you want to push through them.

Sometimes we were riding next to traffic, along the Pacific Coast Highway, sandwiched in between certain death on every side. My vision was better then, and I could see the traffic flying by on one side and the steep drop on the other. So I focused on nothing but the straight ahead and came up with a mantra, something that I'd never even considered before. *Breathe in peace* (breathing in through my nose), *breathe out fear* (breathing out through my mouth). *Breathe in peace, breathe out fear.* It just came out, suddenly there when I needed it. I would go thirty, sixty miles chanting that to myself, almost meditating as I rode. It sticks with me to this day, and in times of stress I've gone back to it. *Breathe in peace, breathe out fear.* It works for me.

At one point there was a hill that was so steep most people had to get off their bikes and walk, but I was determined that I was not going to have to get off my bike. I slowly made my way up, doing my best to breathe in peace, breathe out fear, every muscle in my legs burning. After a while, though, the mantra stopped working, and I started swearing, cursing everything in sight and wondering why I had thought this ride was a good idea, digging my way through each brutal pedal stroke at a turtle's pace. Just when I thought I really wasn't going to be able to do it and I was ready to hop off and walk, I noticed a man wearing very plain-looking clothes—not typical riding gear, which I had stocked up on in the hope that looking the part might help my riding skills—slowly making his way alongside of me. We were both breathing too heavily to acknowledge one another, but, as he drew up next to me, I saw his tall, skinny plastic pole with the little orange flag waving lazily with the breeze. And just below the bottom of the pole was a small sticker that said HIV POSITIVE. I saw no disgust or frustration on his face, only signs of exhaustion and determination to make it to the top. So I mustered up what would have to pass for a grin, but probably looked more like a maniacal grimace, and pedaled on.

I soon realized that I must be close to the top, because I could hear people cheering from not far off. I pushed with all my might and finally crested the hill, where there was a crowd gathered to look at the view cheering, urging us up. I finally got off my bike, exultant, and my legs buckled under me, loose as jelly. I drank deeply from my water bottle and looked at the beautiful vista spread before me, feeling so proud and happy to be there. Then I turned and started cheering for those coming up next, exhausted but exuberant as they, too, made it to the top. It was incredible to see all of those grinning faces and orange flags, even better than the stunning view below us.

After biking for twelve hours at a time for six and a half grueling, exhilarating days, I arrived at the finish line, where my dad, Dan, and two of my best friends, Lisa and Kim, were waiting, cheering me on. I felt triumphant and proud. A part of me couldn't believe that I had just done this all by myself. Of course, I hadn't really been alone, I thought, looking around me at all the flushed, happy faces of others who had just finished. It made me feel independent and strong, and ready for the next big challenge facing me: New York.

26

When I arrived in New York City in mid-August, it felt like a full-on assault. I'd visited once the winter before to look at Columbia's School of Social Work and had been instantly captivated by the city. I had flown in from Southern California, with its hypnotically sunny days, and loved feeling a real season again, having the snow flurry around me as I discovered Manhattan for the first time. I walked uptown, downtown, through Central Park, Rockefeller Center, the West Village. I fell in love, like millions before me, already beginning to dream up my own New York inside me, the sights and sounds and places that would forever change my life and become my home.

August was nothing like the wonderland that had greeted me on my first visit. Anyone who has been to Manhattan in the summer knows the wall of heat and fragrance that immediately hits you, the constant, hazy glare of the sun ricocheting off the buildings, cabs, and concrete. The suffocating heat trapped in the subway stations. The throngs of sweaty people crowded together on the platforms, trying their best to stay fresh and cool on their way to work, long since having given up by the ride home, wilting like dying flowers. Scattering like birds on the weekends, leaving only those unlucky enough not to have the means or the time to escape.

The worst part for me, though, was the stench of garbage: rotting, lining the streets, piled in front of restaurants and apartment buildings, a steamy stew that violated my nostrils on every block. My nose is like the love child of a pregnant woman and a truffle pig, working desperately to make up for my weaker senses, and smells barely noticeable to most can sometimes overwhelm me. I was so nauseated when I first moved to the city that I would often gag when I walked outside, and I found myself missing the gentle heat and happy light of California. I knew, though, that this was where I wanted—where I needed—to be.

I was also hoping that it would help to ease the pain of the things I could no longer do. In New York I could get myself anywhere I needed to go, provided I remembered to carefully check the signs taped up on what seemed like every subway station pole, alerting me to schedule and line changes. I took many an unplanned trip to the Bronx and Brooklyn trying to find my way around, but at least I was doing it on my own.

So here I was, sweating and trying not to smell myself in a city I didn't know, wanting to feel ready to take on the world. I had made it to Columbia! Fuck going deaf and blind, I was going to do this. I was planning for a double master's in social work and public health, and on the first day made my way to the Disability Services office, striding in, looking for the advocates I knew would be there to support me. Except they weren't.

When I asked the bored-looking woman at the front desk of the office about getting texts in a larger font, I got a nod toward the copy machine. When I mentioned finding note takers for my classes, so that I could read the professors' lips during lectures, I was told to make an announcement to each of my classes to see if anyone would be interested in doing it. The last thing I wanted to do was put a spotlight on me, or my disabilities, during the first week of school, before I had even made any friends. To have to be *the girl going blind and deaf* from the very first day. I was beside myself, trying to hold back tears.

I had moved to New York because I wanted to feel completely independent, to do everything on my own. Well, now I was. There was no Joni, no one to call a professor and tell them that they *must* help me. Nobody else was going to do this for me, the same way, after my accident, nobody else could get up and take the first steps for me. The advocate was going to have to be me. Right now, though, I could advocate all I wanted, but that wasn't going to change the disinterested look on the face of the woman who was emphatically not helping me, and it wasn't going to get me a note taker in time for my first class. Vowing that as soon as I had the time I was going to fix this broken system, I gathered up my books and marched over to the copy machine.

27

Right as I felt like I was starting to find my way, Daniel started to lose his. The changes were subtle at first. When I left California he was happy and healthy, or seemed to be. He was at the top of his class in law school, and he never seemed to get stressed out the way other students did. He always had plenty of time for fun, too. I don't think I had ever seen Daniel fail, or do anything less than excel, at anything he set his sights on. And though we had always been physically close, and adored each other, he had never seemed to need me. He just wasn't emotionally needy.

So it was strange when he started to call me more, trying me again and again before I'd have a chance to get back to him. He was talking faster, too, rambling on in what became an increasingly repetitive jumble, seeming desperate to get the words out as quickly as he could. At first, as it became more incomprehensible, I thought part of it was my hearing loss, but then I started to recognize the signs.

The changes in him had been subtle at first, little things I hadn't picked up on that became clearer as time went on. Mental illness runs in my family; I had seen my father go through this more than once, and I was sitting through classes that illuminated its various symptoms and treatments. Daniel kept saying he wasn't happy in law school, that he needed to do something more important, and though he graduated with the highest honors, he never took the bar.

After that, the calls became more intense, and the strange stories began. He heard music coming out of his speakers, even when the stereo was off. "I can make myself levitate," he told me when he called one night, his voice matter-of-fact in the face of this extraordinary news. We knew he had full-blown mania at this point, but even then we had no idea how severe it would get. My parents and I encouraged him to get help, and we did research to try to figure out exactly what he was dealing with.

A few months later, I met him in Los Angeles for a mutual friend's wedding. When he picked me up at the airport the changes in him were immediately clear to me. When I hugged him he smelled different; there was a clear change in his pH, an acridness that hadn't been there before. I got into the car with trepidation. He was still my Danny, but something was very off, not just his smell but his eyes, even more piercing than usual, his exaggerated voice and hand gestures, his clear sense of import in everything he said.

Then he started steering with his feet, so that he could better get his grandiose point across with sweeping hand gestures. We were alone in the car, and I knew I would have felt safer had I been behind the wheel, but there was no way I was going to ask to drive. So, terrified of getting him worked up, I gently cajoled him into putting his hands back on the wheel, nodding and agreeing with whatever point he was making and trying to turn the conversation to something calm and banal.

When I came home to visit a few months later, he somehow managed to convince me to drive with him again. I think that I felt less scared knowing that someone else was in the car with him, even though I knew he drove alone all the time. This time, though, he wouldn't stop at the stop signs, insisting that it didn't matter, that we were safe from all harm, that he and I were above everything. Nobody would hit us, he assured me, because people were all one.

We finally stopped at a burger place for lunch. I got out of the car with shaking legs, wondering how I could have possibly agreed to this and why nobody had stopped him before now. When we walked into the restaurant Daniel sat down and immediately struck up a conversation with a stranger at the next table, asking to share her fries and talking intensely at her. It is a testament to Daniel's extraordinary charisma that she didn't even leave the table but let him sit there, a combination of pity and fascination in her eyes. He would sit down and ramble to homeless people; he got it, he insisted. He understood them, and they understood him, on the high plane on which he now existed. Of course, I was up there with him. He seemed to want and need me more than he ever had, and our twin-ness occupied an ever-larger space in his mind. We were extraordinary, almost gods, unstoppable together. As heartbreaking as it was, a part of me still wanted to laugh as I white-knuckled it home. The unstoppable, godlike half-deaf-and-blind girl and her manic twin brother.

I sensed right away that Danny's illness was just as physical as mine. We now know that mental illness can be both hereditary and genetic, and a huge new study has targeted anomalous genes that show up in a wide variety of mental disorders: schizophrenia, bipolar disorder, autism, major depression, and ADHD. My father has had his troubles, though not with the severity of Dan, but my father lives a full, productive life and is helped by medication.

I knew Daniel had seen doctors and tried the drugs they had prescribed, but he never stayed on them for long. I now know how hard it can be to get a full picture of what someone is going through, because people may only share a part of themselves or talk about only what they believe is an issue. In addition, the medications for bipolar disorder—which seemed to fit most with his symptoms, because there were periods of serious depression between the episodes of mania—dulled my brother's brilliant mind and puffed up his face and body. I have been told over the years by many people that he is the most gorgeous guy they've ever seen, and I'm sure that a few friends feigned more interest in me than they had in order to get closer to him. He had already lost so much, even at that point, that it must have been hard to let go of his beauty, even at that high a cost. One of the hallmarks of his illness, too, was believing that he was *not* sick, which made him even more wary of his medication.

I didn't want to leave him when it was time for me to fly back to New York, somehow believing that if I was there he would be safer. Seeing Daniel like this scared me more than anything in my life ever had, and I prayed that the next time that I saw my brother he would be better.

28

When I was little I wanted to be a veterinarian, before I understood that it was more than just playing with and petting dogs. Daniel wanted to be a professional basketball player. Peter always wanted to be a news anchor, which always struck me as funny. What kid knows that he wants to be a news anchor? He is now a news correspondent for NBC. He *looks* the part perfectly, too, with his strong jaw, perfect hair, blue eyes, and well-modulated, sympathetic voice. I only wish the rest of the world could see the other side of my quick-witted, hysterically funny brother.

My second choice when I was young would have probably been to be an actress. So when I saw flyers up for *The Vagina Monologues* auditions during my first year of social work at Columbia, I figured I'd give it a shot. I decided that I wouldn't tell them about my disabilities, because if I got the part, I wanted it to be totally on my own merit. A part of me was also worried that they wouldn't cast me if they knew, so I just kept quiet about it.

When they called to tell me that I had gotten the part I was over the moon.

When I started at Columbia, I had gone to the health center my first week, knowing that they had an eating disorder team there. I had done an intensive outpatient program, three nights a week, and it had really helped me, and was still helping me, work through my body image issues. When I got the part, though, rehearsals were every night, and I knew that it would mean giving up the program. I weighed my decision carefully, and, though the team urged me not to, I chose the play. The program had been wonderful for me, but I didn't want to feel as though my eating disorder was keeping me from something that I really wanted to do. I soon knew that I had made the right choice.

After I got the part I explained my disabilities, and the director, Dana, was totally unfazed. I was worried that I wouldn't be able to do the scene changes in the dark, but she integrated it into the play, having someone lead me on and off the stage every time I was on. Then she asked me if, for the opening, I would sign along with the narrator. I was thrilled.

I played a few different parts, and my favorite was a little girl in her classroom, showing off her vagina knowledge to her teacher. I played it for laughs and loved hearing the audience roar. Even though I sucked at the dance sequences, it was fantastic. At the end of the show, I stood there with the group of extraordinary women, and though the lights blinded me too much to be able to see the audience, I could hear their wild applause, I felt so proud, so *able*. I never thought I'd be able to do something like that, and it did more for my self-esteem than I could have imagined.

29

There was no way I could ride a bike in New York City. I was already a hazard to myself (and sometimes others) just navigating the streets on foot. My ophthalmologist recommended that I run using a tether with a partner, even in Central Park, to be sure that I'd be safe. There was a group called Achilles International that hosted runs for the blind and provided fully sighted running partners and a tether. I thought it was awesome that the group existed, but I had always preferred to be the one leading the way, not following someone else's lead. But I was desperate for something to help me burn off steam and keep my body strong. So I decided to do what every other New Yorker does: I joined a gym, paying way too much money, profoundly aware of the sculpted perfection around me.

The minute I hopped on the saddle for my first spin class, I fell in love. It didn't hurt my foot or back and left me exhausted and drenched in sweat, feeling fully alive and able in my body. The parts of me that didn't work well seemed to disappear as I pedaled. It didn't matter that I couldn't hear most of what the instructor was saying, which was drowned out by the thumping of the bass, or that, between my limited vision in the dark and the sweat running into my eyes, I couldn't see very well. I didn't need to. I loved the feeling of pushing myself as hard as I could up a steep climb and then pedaling as quickly as I could in a sprint. I was on a bike that went absolutely nowhere, which meant I didn't have to worry about running into anything or anyone. I was able to build my endurance and strength using all of the muscles that I had brought back to life in the years since my accident. I could push myself as hard as anyone else because there was nothing in my way. I had recaptured that feeling of being fully alive in my body, appreciating all of its strength.

We spend so much time thinking about those parts of us that aren't physically perfect, and are so hard on ourselves. Even half-blind I could see that a lot of people here spent as much time watching themselves in the mirror as they did exercising. I'm not immune to it any more than any other woman. I am disappointed with myself when my ass feels too big for my jeans or when I've eaten an entire pint of peppermint-stick ice cream. I can see well enough to notice the perfectly toned woman spinning in front of me with her impossibly straight posture, and I have to work hard not to wonder what she does that I don't in order to look like that. But my accident, as much as my disabilities, helped me to see the power of my own body and how precious it is. When I find something that I love, something that I can do as well as anyone else— without being singled out or noticed for what I can't do, just being one of the group, on equal footing with everybody else—it feels so freeing.

When I realized I needed a part-time job while attending graduate school, teaching spin seemed like the perfect answer. My gym membership would be free, I could play my own music, and I would get paid for doing something I loved. It was a way of performing, which I had always loved. I could motivate people, encourage them to challenge themselves and keep their spirits high. It was my party, and I was thrilled to see my classes packed to capacity every time. I began teaching at New York Sports Club and New York Health and Racquet, then Equinox, the Sports Club/LA, SoulCycle, and Zone Hampton. I would teach fifteen to twenty classes a week even while carrying a full workload. I became an eating, sleeping, studying, and spinning machine, and even though I was maxed out on every front, I loved it.

Over the years I have been amazed at my ability to navigate each dark spin room based on my memory of the studio space. I have gotten good at this in all areas of my life: counting stairs, memorizing familiar places, and even remembering exactly where to go in a grocery store or drugstore to get what I need, so that I don't spend hours wandering around, aimless and lost. When I dance in a class, I know instinctively where there is an open space where I won't trip over something. I know the spin rooms I have taught in for years like the back of my hand, and I could navigate them with my eyes closed. Luckily for me, I don't need to yet.

Of course, spin has its challenges. Like being one of the worst possible environments for a partially sighted and hearing-impaired person. Because it's dark and loud. Really, really loud. And when one of my hearing aid batteries died—which invariably happened, because hearing aid batteries are notoriously shitty batteries—I had to jump off my bike and, while motivating the class and scanning the room for any hands up for help, do a blind search through my backpack, sorting through to find one of the three sizes of batteries to fit whichever aid I was wearing to teach. This was by far the most exhausting part of the class.

As I taught over the years it got more and more difficult. But the exhilaration continued to outweigh the difficulties. At spin I was just Rebecca, the perky instructor who liked to dance in her classes and motivate everyone. I wanted to help people learn what I had: that our bodies are capable of so much more than we give them credit for. That it is most often our own fears that get in our way, and that we hold ourselves back without even knowing it. I knew this firsthand, because I didn't have any choice. It was either that or never learn to walk properly again. That or stay inside, shut out from the rest of the world, because I couldn't see much or hear much. My students didn't need to know about my problems any more than they needed to know that I had graduated from Columbia and was a psychotherapist. They just needed me to cheer them on, push them, encourage them. I was the one helping. I was in the seat I wanted to be in.

. . . .

It's different now. My psychotherapy practice has grown and flourished, which is wonderful, but that's not the only reason why I teach just a few classes a week. I know I'm not as quick as I used to be. I often can't hear what someone's problem is if she needs help, or I can't see if she's waving her hand. Before I became more comfortable telling people that I was visually impaired, I used to tell them that I didn't have my glasses on and to please come up to me if I didn't see their hand in the air.

After class, when people come over to ask questions, which they inevitably do, it takes every bit of focus I have to try to understand what they are asking me, in their out-of-breath voices in the echoing, dimly lit studio. I hate the idea that people may think I'm rude or insensitive if I don't notice them. I was raised to be incredibly polite, and my entire professional life is responding to people's feelings. But I know that I am missing things. That I could offend people, put them off, hurt their feelings.

Recently, I've been more open with the class about my disabilities. A handful of people whom I have become friends with over the years help me negotiate the class, and people have been happy to accommodate me by raising their voices or pointing me in the right direction toward someone who needs help. It can be exhausting to teach a class now, but I still love it, and though I don't have the time to devote to spin that I used to, I'm not giving it up just yet.

30

When I first saw Alan's profile on JDate, in the winter of my last year of graduate school, I remember thinking to myself, *I'm going to marry this guy.* His online profile was full of wit and his sense of humor was unmistakable. He was eight years older than I was, unbelievably funny and clever, and, though not my typical muscle-bound jock, he had an adorable smile and a grown-up menschiness that I found myself instantly attracted to. Though all that I had been through had in some ways given me a maturity that others my age didn't have, there were other ways in which I had given myself license to act less grown-up. While I had dated a lot of guys in college, there had been no one serious, and I realize now that I always had one foot out the door. If I didn't, I reasoned, they probably would. A part of me would wonder how long someone was going to want to stay with me when it sank in that, while I might be very self-sufficient now, someday I was going to need help, and lots of it. How could someone try to imagine a future with a woman who would someday be deaf and blind?

In my better moments I knew that this wasn't true, that I needed to give guys more credit than that, and I also had to admit to myself my other reasons for not wanting to get too close. How long did I have to be young and pretty? How long would I be able to hide my disabilities and just show a shiny exterior? How long would I be able to banter and charm and not say "what" fifty times in a conversation? Already, I said it too much, and it took much more work than it used to for me to seem normal. So I surprised myself on my first date with Alan.

It began inauspiciously enough. He met me in front of my apartment building, and as we walked to the restaurant, the street noise of the city made it impossible for me to hear most of what he was saying. Whatever he had to say, apparently, was quite funny, and at one point he turned to me and said, "You're killing me here, I'm using my best material and you're not laughing."

Then he actually said, "What are you, deaf?" I didn't say anything back, just smiled and laughed, but then as we got to the restaurant and turned to go inside, I walked straight into the glass door. At this point he probably thought I was either on drugs or a complete lunatic, but he kept at it. The final straw was when he held a fork in front of me to take a bite of his food, and I didn't even see it.

Alan is Jewish and, like many of us, comes from a family where food is so much more than sustenance. It is love, intimacy, and sharing. He was sharing his food, and he thought I was ignoring it, refusing his bite. This was unacceptable. So I told him my entire story on our first date. It was the first time I'd ever done that.

My disabilities didn't faze him a bit. He told me that he had been afraid of disabilities when he was younger, that he had grown up in a family that turned their faces away from people who were blind or in wheelchairs, not understanding, or feeling bad or embarrassed or whatever it is that makes so many uncomfortable when they are faced with people with disabilities. I think that some people just don't know how to react. With pity, or maybe a sympathetic smile? Should they try to ignore it? Does it make people see their own mortality? There are so many reasons that it can be scary to see us. I try not to let it offend me or hurt my feelings. It's their issue to resolve, not mine.

But he embraced it wholeheartedly, going home that very night and Googling all he could about Usher syndrome, becoming an avid student, quickly knowing even more than I did. It has remained that way ever since. We started dating in February and became serious quickly. Even though there was a part of me that held back, that had *always* held back and never let any guy in fully, by May we were saying "I love you." And I meant it. I loved him.

31

That same May, I graduated from Columbia, with a master's in social work and another in public health. I was spending the summer working in the Disability Services office at Columbia, which had improved vastly over the three years that I'd been at school. I had pushed them relentlessly to do a better job at meeting students' needs, and the people who ran the office now were extremely competent. Among other things, professors had been taught to do a much better job accommodating students' needs, and all classes mandatory for graduation were now available in wheelchair-accessible buildings. I felt a sense of pride for having been able to help make the school a better, easier place for other students with disabilities. Alan and I were happy, spending our weekends in the Hamptons, and everything in my life seemed to be pointing in the right direction.

Then, at the end of June, Alan saw a lump in his neck one morning as he was shaving. One of his glands had become swollen and hard, and after a week of antibiotics, it was still there, a golf-ball-size lump that wouldn't go away. He went to an ear, nose, and throat specialist, who told him that he should have a needle biopsy, and when the biopsy came back suspicious for Hodgkin's lymphoma, he was scheduled for a full surgical biopsy. His parents flew up from Florida to be there with him, and the night before the surgery we all had dinner together. It was the first time I had ever met them, and I was incredibly nervous and trying as hard as I could to keep up with the conversation. My eyes darted back and forth, and my ears strained, wanting them to like me, to think I was smart and funny and to see how much I loved their son. Of course, they were probably too distracted and worried to even notice.

After Alan's biopsy, I was supposed to leave on my annual vacation with my mother's family, and Alan encouraged me to go and not to worry. A week later he called me in Hawaii. It was Burkitt's lymphoma, non-Hodgkin's. Rare, and extremely aggressive. When he had gotten his diagnosis he had gone alone, without telling anyone, and had a bone marrow biopsy, an EKG, and a PET scan to determine that his cancer was still stage one. I wished so much that I had been there with him. I knew what it felt like to be alone with a shocking diagnosis.

Alan being Alan, by which I mean a massive control freak as well as a huge science and medicine buff, he took control immediately. Not only did he interview several doctors, but he did a ton of research on his own as well. He found the best specialists, studied the different treatments, and crunched the numbers. He decided to receive treatment that would require nine months of aggressive chemotherapy at the Weill Cornell Medical Center.

The first couple of times he had chemo were going to be inpatient, so I went ahead of him and decorated his room. I remembered how much I had hated being in the hospital and wanted to make it less horrible for him if I could. I decided on a restaurant theme and put a sign on his door that said CHEZ PINTO. I made MADAME and MONSIEUR bathroom signs, and drew pictures of candles and a roast chicken to put on the walls. I brought place settings and Turkish food, wanting to bring his favorites, not knowing how the chemo would affect his appetite, and slept in a chair next to his bed that night. As soon as the first round was over I could immediately smell the difference in him. He had a chemical odor, medicinal and metallic, and I could smell it on his breath and seeping out of his skin.

We went home to his one-bedroom apartment, where his parents were staying, too. They were going to be flying up for every treatment, so he had bought a bed to put in his living room, and for much of the next year it would often be the four of us staying in one small New York City apartment, sharing one bathroom. His mom, whom he calls Suze, was the ideal Jewish mother. She would cook huge Sephardic meals, completely taking over the kitchen to make all of his favorite foods. I shouldn't say "taking over," actually, because I couldn't cook at all. I still can't. I wanted to be able to do these things for him, too, to be able to cook and clean and take care of him, and also to show her that I wasn't completely incapable in the kitchen, so one afternoon I decided that I would bake cookies. Just simple chocolate chip, and the cut-and-bake kind at that. It was something nobody could screw up—except me. I bustled around the kitchen self-importantly, trying to look competent. Somehow, though, they ended up completely burned on the bottom and raw on top. Plus, I burned my arm and managed to set the fire alarm off, filling the entire apartment with acrid smoke. Needless to say, she wasn't very impressed.

People were sometimes surprised that I stayed with him, since we had been together for such a short time, but it never occurred to me not to. We never know everything that's coming, and life can change in an instant. I have had plenty of experience with being dismissed as a potential girlfriend or partner because of my disabilities, and that wasn't something I was ever going to do to somebody else.

When my summer job ended, instead of looking for another one right away, I thought I was supposed to stay with him. It was my first adult relationship, and I didn't know quite how to act. I wanted to be brave and good and there for whatever he needed, and I thought maybe I should do that at the expense of everything else. I sat through his chemo sessions with him, and we watched every episode of *Lost*. He was amazing. Though I knew he was constantly nauseous, exhausted, and in pain, he tried never to let it show, and he never lost his sense of humor.

After a little while, though, it became clear that it wasn't working for me to be around all the time. Alan is a natural helper and giver, and suddenly we had two caretakers in the relationship, neither of whom were good at letting someone else help them. Our first big fight happened that fall, when he told me in no uncertain terms that I needed to get a job and stop sitting around his apartment. He didn't like being taken care of, and knew how hard I'd worked to get my degrees, and didn't want me held back in any way by his illness.

· · · ·

I soon began working at St. Francis de Sales School for the Deaf, in Brooklyn, as the school social worker. The children there were all ages, from toddlers to eighth graders, and many were immigrants and came from poor backgrounds. I would meet with the families of the children, helping them navigate Medicaid or find employment and deal with family issues. Many of the parents didn't know how to sign, other than the very rudimentary basics, so I would often find myself interpreting between them and their children. These parents would come to me not understanding why their ten-year-old had started throwing huge fits in the house. My heart broke for these kids, and I tried to educate the parents while swallowing my feelings of fury: Imagine not being able to communicate your feelings to your own family, and not having parents able to understand the thoughts and curiosity of their child's growing mind.

There were sign classes for adults before and after school, and I urged the parents to take them so that they could communicate with their kids. I watched how much more well-adjusted the children who had deaf parents or parents who signed were, and the ease with which they managed the world, and I realized that it really *didn't* have to be a disability. If they were part of a strong deaf community, they could all live full, happy, and productive lives.

That was when I started to make more deaf friends and to spend more time in the deaf community. Though I had a very small field of vision, what I had was clear and strong with the help of contacts or glasses, which could correct for my nearsightedness, and when I gave someone my full attention, I could be fully engaged in a conversation. It also felt easier to tell them about my eyes. Many of them were familiar with Usher syndrome, and it felt like a great burden was lifted when I could just fully be myself, unjudged, and communicate in a language in which I felt entirely comfortable.

. . . .

After Alan's nine months of chemo, his cancer was gone, and he could fully return to his life. Our relationship, however, which had felt like it was on hold in many ways during that past year, despite how much time we'd spent together, was already showing signs of strain.

32

After four years on and off together, trying again and again to make it work, Alan and I finally broke up, but we have never stopped being friends. In fact, he's still one of the people closest to me in the world, and I think that if most people in my life had their way, I would end up with him. It's hard to breach the inner circle of my closest friends and family, but Alan busted through with charm and ease. He now *is* family. It would be perfect, in a fantasy world.

While I can honestly say that we are much better, and happier, as friends than we were as a couple, sometimes I worry that he has set the bar too high for other men. He knows everything there is to know about me and loves me absolutely. Who could ever know me the way he does—not just my disabilities, but all of my flaws and issues, too—and still love me so completely? How often do you find someone who can really love you for exactly who you are? He still wants to fix me; he'll *always* want to fix me—not because he thinks I'm broken, but because he sees how difficult going deaf and blind can be and he wants me to enjoy everything that fully sighted and hearing people do.

I also can't imagine someone who would be a better father than Alan. He is awesome with kids, loving and warm and just what a child would want in a dad, what any woman would want for the father of her children.

He gets me, too. That was one of the most wonderful things about our relationship. We had so much fun, and we were constantly laughing. We still make each other laugh. He likes my offbeat sense of humor, and he makes sure to repeat anything I miss that he knows I would think was funny. He took me to *The Book of Mormon* recently and spent half of it retelling me the jokes.

He brings me wildly expensive boxes of imported saffron because he read that it improves retinal function, and bombards me with supplements and information and optimism. He meets with every doctor doing retinal research, often accompanied by my dad, and follows every trial. He attends conferences about blindness and follows every lead and bit of science, with Google Alerts set up to notify him of the tiniest bit of news that could affect me. I'm so glad he does this, because it means I don't have to, and truthfully, I wouldn't anyway. While of course I would love for there to be a cure—and I helped to organize an annual Usher III Initiative benefit, Spin-for-Sight, that raised $110,000 in its inaugural event—I have no real interest in following the science until it becomes close to a possibility for me. I trust that he and the rest of the people who are close to me will tell me when anything important comes along. He is paternal, a fixer, and an eternal optimist.

For all of this, there are many reasons that we didn't, ultimately, work as a couple. Many of them were my fault. I was young, and self-centered in so many ways. Some out of necessity, and some because I just wasn't ready, didn't know how to be a girl-friend, didn't know how to take love seriously. Alan always wanted to fix me, to help me fix myself, to save me. He urged me toward clinical trials that I wasn't ready for. When you've got a disability like mine, a lot of the men you attract are going to be control freaks and father figures. Alan, though he is one of my favorite people on this earth, has got his fair share of both.

A lot of it, too, was just timing, which really can be every-thing, and you can't change it any more than you can change the weather. Alan and I had the wrong timing for romance, but we have the best timing for friendship. He is the most supportive friend I could imagine, and goes so above and beyond what friendship probably means to many people that I almost don't even have a word to describe him. He is family, really. He is a rock, and I can't imagine my life without him.

I wonder sometimes if he fills too many of the needs that I have, and if it would be easier to accept another man fully into my life if I didn't have him. I don't know. I know that he wants me to find someone, he's made that very clear over the years, though, for him, too, ours was the longest and most serious rela-tionship he'd ever had.

I know this, though: Whether or not it makes it harder for me to be in a serious relationship, I am not giving Alan up. No chance. I can admit now what I couldn't then: I need him.

33

People often tell me that I don't look like a "disabled person." Sometimes when I bring my dog, Olive, wearing her service vest, down into the subway station, I get a look and a raised eyebrow from the station agent, and I've been stopped plenty of times. It usually goes something like this:

"Is this a seeing eye dog?" (casting a doubtful eye on the little, curly-haired dog wagging her tail next to me).

"She's a service dog."

"Are you blind?" (asked skeptically).

"I'm visually impaired."

"Really?" (even more skeptically).

"Yes, I'm also hearing impaired" (lifting my hair to show my hearing aids).

"Hmmm. Okay. You don't look disabled."

At this point I'm never sure what to say. Um, thanks? What's the appropriate response here? I usually settle for a smile and go on my way, hoping that Olive doesn't do anything to make us look like frauds.

After being told hundreds of times that I don't look disabled or blind, I'd really like to ask people: What does it look like? For a long time I was able to hide my disabilities, whether it was intentional or not. Now that I can no longer conceal them, I'm starting to think it will be easier. Part of me doesn't want that to be the first thing people know about me, to have my disabilities be the starting point, but it's so exhausting to try to hide or correct for them. It seems that in New York, especially, we size each other up awfully fast. Clothes, shoes, bag, job, neighborhood, boom! But we have no idea what each of us is carrying inside.

34

Caroline's first impression of me was not a good one. In fact, she couldn't stand me. She worked at the desk at Zone Hampton NYC, one of the spin studios where I taught, and is not a morning person, to say the least. I would bounce in to teach my six fifteen A.M. spin class, chirp a singsong "Gooooood morrrrn-ing!" and try to strike up a conversation with her. She would give me a look that said she clearly thought I was insane, a look that she gives me to this day—though now it makes me laugh. Then she would mumble a grudging hello and go back to studying, hunching over her book, her blond hair a curtain around her face, her slender collarbone jutting out from above her shirt the only part of her exposed.

It was clear that she had no interest in me, but for reasons I still can't quite explain I was drawn to her. Even then I could see glimpses of her dry sense of humor when she greeted other people. When I focused in on her face I could see a sharpness in her pale blue eyes that seemed to catch everything, and, even more than that, a recognition of something in them that lived inside of me, too, a part that I never showed other people, that I worked so hard to try to defeat. A lack of comfort with herself, a turning in, as if she didn't want the world to see her and didn't like what she herself saw.

I have always made friends easily, but with Caroline I had to work at it. I was relentless, stopping at the desk to chat between my classes, asking her about herself, leaning over to see what she was reading. Finally one morning she held up her Spanish textbook with a sigh. This was great, I told her. I had always wanted to learn Spanish! If she would teach it to me, I would teach her sign language. To my delight and surprise, she agreed.

Maybe she just gave in, accepting that this crazy person wasn't going to leave her alone until she did, or maybe part of her was glad that I was trying so hard to be her friend, since she needed one more than she ever let on at the time. Whatever it was, I thank the universe for bringing us together, because Caroline is the best friend I have ever had. She is my Annie Sullivan, but she tells me that I saved her and that I helped bring her back into the world.

I didn't tell her about my disabilities right away, and maybe she thought all of my "What?"'s and "What was that?"'s were part of a general flightiness. I wanted to, but sometimes it's difficult to try to figure out where and when to fit it into a conversation. I didn't want everyone I worked with to know all about it, though a few weeks later, there was an article about me in *New York* magazine, and I knew that cat was going to be out of the bag. So I preempted it, tossing a copy as casually as I could on her desk the day it came out and dodging immediately into my class.

The next time that I saw her she was a little awkward, doing the look-away shuffle and the "If there's anything I can do" mumble, two classic responses. I was finally relaxed about it, though. Being honest just feels *better;* it's not nearly as exhausting as keeping things in, which is just so much work, and my honesty would eventually help her open up to me about things that she generally didn't talk about. Best of all, we realized that we had the same absurd sense of humor.

I was hanging out by her desk one afternoon in between classes, still unsure whether or not she kind of thought of me as a nuisance, and she made some obvious observation about something, to which I retorted, "Does a snake drag its balls?"

Caroline looked up sharply. "What?"

"Does a one-legged duck swim in circles?" I continued.

She started to laugh and couldn't stop, a sound I had never heard from her before. She told me later that she felt something that she hadn't in a long, long time. *This is what having a friend feels like.*

At first, Caroline hadn't told me much about herself. Like that she was an accomplished violinist who had been playing since she was a young child. Or that she had spoken to almost no one her entire freshman year of college, feeling so out of place and different from her peers that she retreated into herself and her studies and moved back to New York after a year to be closer to her parents, and continued school in the city. Or that she had been anorexic, paralyzed by the need for control and order that so many of us face. Worst of all, she had no one to laugh with, which, since we laugh together every single day, is simply unimaginable to me.

It was like we filled a void in one another, and once we started spending time together I could no longer imagine my life without her. She started learning sign, and we could soon communicate in a language that is often much easier for me. I encouraged her to become a spin instructor and told her that she didn't belong behind the desk, and she started her training.

. . . .

One morning, several months after Caroline and I had gotten close, I bounced into the gym with my usual cheerful enthusiasm and found her looking even more unhappy than her usual morning self. In fact, she looked downright depressed. When I asked her what was wrong, she glumly replied that she wasn't going to be able to go home for Easter that year, between work and exams. Holidays were a very, *very* big deal in Caroline Kaczor's household, and as an only child, she was devastated at the prospect of spending Easter away from her parents. What about her personalized egg hunt on the hill overlooking Three Mile Harbor on Long Island? What about the beautiful basket full of goodies she always received? she asked wistfully, missing the fun of childhood and her parents, irritated with all of the adult responsibilities weighing on her. Caroline's not a complainer, so I could tell that it was really important to her, even if the whole thing sounded pretty silly to me.

So I bought her an Easter basket and filled it with every candy that I knew she loved, and brought it to the studio that Easter Sunday. I knew that she would be sitting behind the desk, frowning down at her schoolwork, so when the elevator doors opened I held the basket up over my face and walked to the desk. Her look was priceless. You would have thought that she had just won the lottery by the way she jumped up and down and grabbed the basket from me. As I watched her rifle happily through it, delighting at the jellybeans, the Reese's peanut butter eggs, and the chocolate bunnies, I felt so happy to have been able to do something for her that meant so much.

One day a few months later I was teaching back-to-back classes and then had meetings for the rest of the day, and I found myself downtown in the pouring rain, with just a little time before my next meeting, ravenous. I had forgotten my wallet, and I called Caroline, trying to laugh at my predicament but unable to at that point. I can't function without food. My days are often jam-packed, and when I am low on fuel, I am even more of an accident waiting to happen than usual. I could deal with the rain, the hectic schedule, my eyes and ears and everything else, but the idea of doing it all on an empty stomach had completely defeated me. Caroline thought for a moment, and then she directed me to the nearest Starbucks, went on their website and bought a gift card, and immediately emailed it to me. Five minutes later I was sitting inside, warm and dry, drinking coffee and eating oatmeal.

Sometimes, friendship requires very little. A coffee, a chat, a small favor. An Easter basket or an emergency gift card to Starbucks. Our deepest friendships require more. They are not bound by blood or marriage, but forged freely. They need to be nourished, but the lines are blurry; there is no contract, nothing to say what it means to be a good friend. We decide for ourselves what it means. We may lose touch and reconnect; we may find that a friendship no longer works or that we've "outgrown" one.

My friendships are life sustaining. Without Caroline and Alan and Lisa and my other closest friends, my world would be so much darker and quieter, so much less humorous and joyful, and so much harder. For me, even a small thing can be huge. Caroline has found one of my dropped pearl earrings more times than I can count. If I break a glass in my apartment, there's no way that I am going to be able to find all the little shards, so I clean up as much as I can see, then retreat to my bedroom with Olive, so we don't cut ourselves, and call Caroline, who will come over as quickly as she can to help.

Sometimes I hate having to do this, to always be the one who's going to need more help than anyone else. When I'm especially frustrated with myself for feeling so needy, I think of Helen.

When people hear "blind and deaf," I know that their frame of reference is probably Helen Keller. Brave, pioneering Helen, who learned the world through her hands and the love and patience of one extraordinary woman, Annie Sullivan, her miracle worker. Through Annie, Helen learned a world that she had no understanding of. I am losing the senses that she never remembered having.

Helen was so grateful for what she had. "My life has been happy because I have had wonderful friends and plenty of interesting work to do," she once remarked, adding, "I seldom think about my limitations, and they never make me sad. Perhaps there is just a touch of yearning at times, but it is vague, like a breeze among flowers. The wind passes, and the flowers are content."

Helen's life is a beacon of inspiration and a story that people continue to be drawn to. She rose above what at that time were insurmountable odds to become a writer, a political activist, and an inspiring speaker and lecturer. It was her Annie, though, who made that life possible, who spent her life freely with Helen so that she could come to know the world and share her extraordinary self with it. They were together for forty-nine years. Half a century! I, too, have to have faith that my friends wouldn't be here if they didn't want to be, and that they love me as much as I love them.

35

I stared at the screen, chewing on my fingernails, then stopped, remembering how Caroline always batted my hands away in disgust when I did. Then I started chewing again.

I had filled out the countless questions about myself over the years: what my perfect date would be, my body type, eye color, favorite books, political leanings, sexual preferences, thoughts on religion. So many questions that when my eyes couldn't focus anymore Caroline had sat there answering them for me, generally stating the answer rather than asking me for it; she knows me well enough to do a better job than I would.

Those dating sites get pretty personal, sort of. You may have an awful lot of info about someone, from his past drug use to how many times a week he likes to have sex, but everybody is putting his or her best foot forward: Their most tanned and toned pictures show up, generally taken a few years (or more) ago, and flaws listed are generally along the lines of "I expect too much of myself."

But, of course, there's even more left off of the page: I take Zoloft. I ejaculate prematurely. Probably because of my parents' fucked-up marriage, I've never had a girlfriend for more than three months. I'm an inveterate cheater. I lied about my drug history. Or how about this one? I'm going blind and deaf.

Dating is complicated for most of us. Navigating the delicate dance of romance, with all of its unwritten laws and complexities: When do you text, phone, show up with nothing but lingerie under your coat? And the process of really getting to know someone: How soon do you put all your cards on the table?

For me, this process can be exponentially more difficult. For one, I'm not usually able, even with my hearing aids, to catch everything someone says, and on a date it's often too dark to read lips. So I can say nothing and look like an idiot, and, even worse, not laugh at his jokes. Or I can tell him, reveal all immediately: *Hey, it's great to meet you, you're super cute—and oh, by the way, there's probably something you should know.* And if not right away, how long do I wait? These days, a Google search is de rigueur when you meet someone, and guess what's going to show up if you search under my name? Articles about my living with Usher syndrome, and me on the *Today* show, talking to Meredith Vieira. I'm told it's an inspiring piece, but it's tough to lead with.

It's happened more than once. One night I was introduced to a funny, adorable guy at a party; we had a great time and went on a fantastic date a few days later. Somehow we got on the subject of languages, and I told him that I knew sign language and that I was hearing impaired. He seemed cool with it, and we agreed to go out again.

The next morning I got a very long, honest email from him. Apparently he had Googled me when he went home the night before, and he told me that, despite our chemistry and common interests, my disabilities were too much for him to handle. He had a lot of stress in his life, and it was too much for him to consider taking on.

About forty emotions ran through me at once, indignation and frustration taking the early lead. I hadn't asked him to "take on" anything, I was still just basking in the happiness of a great first date. Then I felt sad and lonely: This was one of my biggest fears—being rejected because of my disabilities, and where they would eventually lead. It wasn't the first time, and it certainly wouldn't be the last. Finally, I just felt a wistful acceptance: He was honest with me, and really, that's all I could ask of him. I didn't blame him for feeling that way, and who knows, maybe I would have, too, if I'd been in his shoes. And who am I to judge? God knows I've rejected plenty of guys for far less. As Alan had recently said when he'd IM'd me, chiding me for being too critical and dismissing profiles for the smallest irritations, "I bet you never thought you'd fall in love with a balding, chubby guy with cancer." He wasn't wrong. There was no guy I had ever loved more than Alan.

We never know what life is going to throw at us, and I can't deny that I wanted this man who so easily dismissed me to think I was worth taking that risk for. Would I have been if we'd gone on a few more dates before he found out? What about if we had been friends first, if he'd watched how I handled my disabilities, seen how rich and full and happy my life was despite them?

Seated there on my couch, Olive curled up next to me, trying to nudge away my computer so that she could take full control of my lap, I was about to take one of those chances. I was going to update my profile to add that I wore hearing aids. I didn't know how many guys would dismiss me as a potential love interest because of it or who would read that far down into my profile to notice, but I thought I owed them, and myself, at least some honesty up front. I heard my mother's voice in my head: "Be up-front, who wouldn't want you? Why would you want them if they wouldn't want you for who you are? You're my beautiful, brilliant

Rebecca." The usual Jewish-mom stuff. But she had a point. She actually thought that I should include a link to the *Today* show piece from my profile, really put it all out there. Caroline thought so, too, as did Alan. I thought about Alan on our first date and the exasperated look on his face when I hadn't laughed at his jokes, and I knew that they were probably right. Look what had happened when I'd just been up-front with him. But I knew that Alan was different from most other people. And, as I reflected on that, I realized that this really wasn't a good time to start thinking about him. Right now the hearing aids seemed like enough of a step.

I knew that even putting it up there might invite in another kind of guy: the kind who needed to be needed or who liked to be controlling. I had already met plenty of those. It irritated me a little that other people could hide their issues in a way that I couldn't, and I knew that if I could still hide mine I probably would, at least until someone got to know me a little bit, but people could tell almost right away that something was off. At first it might seem as though I was just buzzed or distracted, but pretty quickly it became clear that I wasn't the same in person as when we'd texted or emailed. Then I could be quick and witty, and not have to ask a guy to repeat himself constantly or bump into things as we made our way to a table. Or miss the encouraging or naughty things he whispered in my ear, if it came to that. It's an awkward time to ask someone to speak up.

A part of me thought it would be so great if we could all just be completely honest with one another, right off the bat, if we could all just put our shit right out there. But who could? As I added this little factoid about myself and clicked to update my profile, I felt proud of myself. A small coming out, maybe, but it felt big.

36

Caroline and I balance each other out. She is perfectly organized and diligent. I can be both of those things, but I'm also sillier, dreamier, more prone to dancing down the street spontaneously. I bring out her inner goofball, who is always just dying to get out, and she's taught me that keeping myself organized is imperative to making my life easier—and to getting places on time, which has never been my strong suit. When it can take hours to find your keys, it is idiotic not to train yourself to put them in exactly the same place *every time*.

When I go to her house, she carefully puts my stuff on a table that is just for me. When I start to say, "Caroline, where—" I can't even get the words out before she cuts me off with a "Before you ask for anything, confer with the table." She has a caddy for me in her bathroom with contact solution, eye makeup remover, a toothbrush and toothpaste, a brush—all the things I could possibly need. She has extra cases for my hearing aids and all three kinds of batteries for them. She even carries around extra batteries in case I run out. Everybody should have a Caroline: organizer of life, cleaner-upper of broken glass, tactile-signer, and sweet, funny bestie. She even tweezes my eyebrows for me and finds other errant hairs I have a hard time seeing. This is exceedingly important. I cannot have granny whiskers, and she keeps an eye out for them. She can be a little anal, though. Sometimes I think someone watching us would think that we were reenacting a scene from *The Odd Couple*. Like with the nail polish.

One afternoon we were in my apartment, and I was hunting around for a bottle of red nail polish. Everyone in New York gets manicures and pedicures—they're a staple, and there's practically a salon on every block—but I like to do my own. It relaxes me. I'm terrible at sitting still and it gives my hands something to do and keeps me from biting my nails. Also, I want to be able to paint them while I still can (though I'm pretty sure I'm getting worse at it).

So while I was hunting for my nail polish she started to look, too, and found me one. Then another, and another, and then it was on, as she single-mindedly searched my apartment for what turned out to be a really embarrassing number of nail polishes in what could be described as pretty much the exact same shade of red.

"I always think I've lost one," I said in my defense, "and then I need a new one." Caroline raised her eyebrows skeptically. "I'm mostly blind, you know," I continued, determined not to look like a hoarder. But I could see it in her eyes. She continued gathering them up until she had them all in one big snarky pile on the floor and then slowly counted, out loud, as she put them neatly into a big Ziploc baggie. The final count (according to her; like I was going to count) was thirty-two.

"What if I can't find the bag?" I asked, just to be obnoxious. She showed me the drawer where she was putting the nail polish.

"The bag lives here," she told me with finality. I think I was supposed to be learning a lesson, but what I was really thinking was that I'm so glad to have a best friend like Caroline who, even if she is a little annoying about it, would take care of shit like this for me. Someone who would always do things to make my life easier when I needed her to, and, even more important, taught me to do them for myself.

37

When I had finished my training at the American Institute for Psychoanalysis, where I received my certification in psychodynamic psychotherapy, I decided that I was ready to start my own practice. I knew that it would mean being completely self-reliant professionally and that nobody could hold me back except myself. I also knew that I faced extra challenges because of my disabilities, but I couldn't let that stop me.

My very first patient was a woman I'd seen at the Renfrew Center, an eating disorder recovery program that I had worked at briefly, who came to me as soon as she was discharged. I had sectioned off a part of my apartment for an office, and before she came I made sure that it was clean and welcoming, scanning again and again in case I had missed anything. After I began seeing her, word spread and referrals came in, and so I began by specializing in young women with eating disorders, which, with my experience, was a great way to start.

Working with young women, I was constantly reminded of why these issues plague us. It's not about the food. For many, it's about being able to control something, when there is so much that is out of our control. While other people's stories may not seem as dramatic as mine—I have no control over losing two senses that most would consider vital to living a full and happy life—every one of us lives in a world that is full of things that we cannot change, and it can make us feel so strong and empowered to be able to keep our outside looking good when inside we can feel so powerless.

We are also constantly exposed to totally unrealistic messages and beliefs about what a woman should look like, so it's no wonder so many of us fall prey to them. When I walk down the street now, I have hearing aids, and often a cane, and it took a long time for me to work through feeling self-conscious about it. It's hard for me to imagine that a guy is going to check out a girl with a cane and think, *Damn, she's hot,* no matter how good I look, when there are thousands of beautiful women in New York City with no cane or hearing aids and a perfect exterior that hides whatever's underneath. I know I can't worry about that, though, because where is it going to get me, except to make me feel bad and to keep me from using the tools at my disposal to make my life easier and more navigable? I also have to remember that we all have our shit, and it's going to come out and show itself eventually, even if mine is out there earlier than most.

So, it's not about the food. When I finally realized that, it truly was a revelation. It doesn't mean that I don't sometimes feel gross after eating a huge meal or that I don't mind when I look in the mirror and see that I've gained a few pounds, but I can honestly say that I worked mightily to have what is now a healthy relationship with, and appreciation for, both food and exercise.

When I finish a tough workout, I feel as though I could conquer anything. I love food, and I can now fully give myself over to the joy and nourishment that I get from it. My eating disorder no longer has control of me.

. . . .

With two of my senses vastly diminished, I cherish the others, and now, the tactile delight of food and eating is one of my greatest pleasures. I think I may actually love food more than anyone I've ever met. I'm sure other people think that they do, but I'm pretty sure that this is one that I win. I love to really taste and savor the food I eat, and I am the best dinner guest, because I will compliment the food with every bite if I love it. I can't help myself, though I try to wait until I'm done chewing my bite.

Food is a pleasure that is completely unreliant on sight and sound: I love the smoothness of sweet mint ice cream, cool and creamy on my tongue, and the delightful interruption of a tiny pop of peppermint crunch, the little explosion of flavor as it gives under my teeth. Who decided that peppermint-stick ice cream should be a mostly seasonal delight? It is the most delicious and refreshing of ice cream flavors, and if you're a true believer, nothing else is quite the same.

I love the toothiness of a kale salad, tangy with vinaigrette and peppered with crunchy bits of almond and a sweet note of apple, some avocado thrown in there for a contrasting, smooth richness. And nothing beats my mother's famous spaghetti sauce. When I walk into the kitchen and it's full of the smell of warm tomatoes, onions, and oregano, my mouth starts watering as much as Olive's, and I'll eat it over my mom's shoulder, right from the pot. Same with my dad's applesauce. The first bite is like a thousand sweet apples bursting in my mouth at once. Soft black licorice? Hand over the whole bag.

My sense of taste, along with my sense of smell and texture, has gotten so powerful that there are many things that I can't eat that I used to. Meat in any form completely grosses me out, and while I know that fish is something that I should eat, the smell of it cooking makes me gag. Spicy foods are too much for me, and any strong cheeses. If I don't like something, I can't even fake it; it immediately shows on my face.

All of my senses are amplified even more if I have my eyes closed. When Caroline and I treat ourselves to ice cream or frozen yogurt, chock-full of toppings, we eat it with our eyes closed. I have often thought that *The Blind Diet* would be a very marketable book. You tend to slow down, taste things more, savor them. I find it helps me to stop eating not by judging the amount in my bowl, but by noticing when the food stops tasting so delicious and I'm no longer hungry. Not that I always stop there, especially not when it comes to something like ice cream, but I try. It adds so much to the appreciation of my food, and I think anyone's senses are heightened by the loss, voluntary or not, of another one, though I'm probably more adept than most at eating without seeing much. I still knock over glasses all the time, but in the pitch dark, I win every time. Alan and I once went to a dinner for the Foundation Fighting Blindness that was done completely in the dark, and while he struggled to get his food from plate to mouth, finally giving up and holding his meat by the bone to eat it, I managed to steal most of his mashed potatoes, which were even more delicious in the dark.

. . . .

My practice grew quickly, and I soon began seeing deaf patients, who were relieved to find a therapist who understood what it meant to be deaf but also knew that being deaf did not define them. I have a deaf couple who come in and fight in my office, their hands moving so fast and faces and expressions so animated and changing so quickly that I often have to slow them down, unable to keep up with the war zone of flying hands.

I have another patient, a composer who is losing his hearing. I try to imagine what that is like, to be going deaf when your whole world is oriented around your hearing. I teach him sign while we talk, though for him, I know it won't be enough. He isn't just losing his hearing; he's losing his passion, his life's work.

I have patients from India, Colombia, and Singapore, which, as one can imagine, presents its own difficulties. I need to be open and direct about my hearing loss with them, and they are usually more than willing to wear the microphone that works with my hearing aids. I actually think this gives them a sense of empowerment. I cannot practice the way that many of the analysts I was trained under do, which is to not share any information about themselves with patients. That is not a possibility for me.

My practice has to be dynamic, and it has to be a two-way relationship, because if I am not open about my disabilities, I can't do my job, which is to focus on my patients entirely and be totally present for them. People like to feel needed, and my patients have been happy to accommodate me.

. . . .

I love hearing other people's stories, and being able to focus entirely on someone else's needs and what I can do to help them. I have a true understanding of what it means to take each day as it comes, with its joys and sorrows and complications, and to make the most of it. It sounds like something written on a greeting card, but it's true. If I can help my patients to do that, to be truly present in their lives, then I believe my work is worthwhile.

38

In college, when I experienced my first dramatic loss of hearing and the tinnitus started, I couldn't stand to have my hearing aids out, because it made the tinnitus worse. I remember learning about amputees experiencing a "phantom limb"—the sensation that an amputated or missing limb is still attached and moving appropriately with other body parts—and that people who experience it often feel as though the missing limb or body part is distorted or in a painful position. That was as close as I could come to a comparison; my ear couldn't hear, but my brain believed it could and stuck me with the most annoying, painful sound it could find.

A few years after getting my masters' and starting my psychotherapy practice, I was living alone in an alcove studio apartment in New York City. By that time, I had acclimated considerably to my hearing loss. So much so in fact that I looked forward to going home so that I could "take my ears out." As difficult as it is to be hearing impaired, there is nothing better than turning off all of the noise and unnecessary sounds around me. Taking my hearing aids out allows me to focus without distraction, or to re-lax completely, anywhere I am. And there are no babies who sleep as soundly as I do. It is a gift. Not one I would have asked for, but a gift nonetheless.

Then suddenly, all of that changed. Instead of looking forward to going home so that I could take my ears out, I began to dread it. At first I didn't understand that I was beginning to experience a different form of tinnitus. I'd grown so used to the ringing that I mostly just tuned it out. I'm not sure whether this was just my hearing loss progressing further or simply a side effect of the loss I'd been enduring over time, but there was a yearlong period where I experienced serious auditory hallucinations, some of which would last for a week or two, others for several months at a time. All of them started at night, when all I wanted was to be sleeping in my usual uninterrupted bliss.

The midnight jackhammer was the earliest sound I can remember, waking me in the middle of the night, practically rattling my windows. How could workers possibly be jackhammering at this hour? *This city is too fucking much for me,* I thought as I threw my covers off, grumbling to myself about needing to move back to California immediately, and stormed over to the window. With all of the irritation I could muster, I lifted the window open in one quick jolt and leaned out, looking both ways. Was this a joke? There were no workers and no jackhammers on the street—just the steady flow of traffic moving through the light and onto the 59th Street Bridge.

Then the sounds moved indoors and got eerier. Just the kind of stuff a woman living alone wants to hear.

I was lying in my bed one night early in the fall, and the weather was still fairly warm, so I often slept with my window open a little to feel the slow, cool breeze from outside. As I drifted off,

I was quickly startled awake by the sound of knocking. At first I thought it was something outside and closed the window, but then it seemed that it was coming through the wall behind my bed that I shared with my neighbors. I didn't know the layout of their apartment or whether their bed was propped up against the same wall as mine was, so I lay there in the dark imagining every possible scenario in which mysterious knocking played itself out. It sounded so real to me that it felt as though I could hear the reverberation of each knock against my eardrum. Initially, I ignored it and assumed it was not intended for me. But the knocking continued. I decided to knock back on the wall. The neighbors were a young engaged couple who had recently moved in—maybe they were just being silly. It's sort of funny to be so physically close to your neighbors, separated by merely a wall. So strange in the city, where you can live within a couple of feet of people and not even know their names. I knocked back with reluctance. I heard another pattern of knocks so I decided to knock back again, with a bit more confidence and enthusiasm.

Then I had a sudden thought that perhaps it wasn't knocking at all, but the sound of their headboard hitting the wall. That scenario made a lot more sense. I quickly pulled the covers over my head to hide, humiliated. My neighbors were surely getting it on and I seemed like I was trying to participate.

As the night grew later and then earlier into the morning, I started to doubt this theory. Not even twentysomething soon-to-be-marrieds could keep it up for this long! I took a few more guesses about where the knocking was coming from. Plucking the sharpest knife that I could out of my eight-year-old Bed Bath and Beyond knife block, which was probably too dull to cut an apple with, I crept to the door and looked through the keyhole. Nothing. I gripped the handle of the knife more firmly, unlocked my door as quietly as I could, and pulled it open. *En garde!* Still nothing. I looked left and right before stepping out the door to look down the hallway where it turned. Not a soul. After three or four nights of this, I finally fell asleep out of sheer exhaustion, still not realizing that it was all in my head.

The haunting continued. If I had to guess, I would have said that the person walking up the stairs was an adult. Although the footsteps weren't particularly loud or heavy, the stairs were desperately creaky. Each step sounded as though the worn wooden step beneath it could go at any second. But what stairs? I would run out to the hallway, but it was an elevator building, and there was no one on the fire escape stairs. Then what could it be? Again, mystified, I returned to my apartment, trying to sleep through the creaks but unable to silence the part of me that was well aware that this noise was a signal in every horror movie that something is about to jump out and *kill*.

The most frightening sound came last. A woman's scream. Like the other sounds, the scream woke me suddenly in the middle of the night. It was terrified and piercing, and sent an echoing chill through my entire body. Like all of the other sounds, I experienced the screams as though they had physically penetrated my eardrums. My visceral response was to curl into a ball and pull the covers over my head to hide. While squeezing my eyes shut, I put my hands over my ears, trying desperately to block out the noise, wondering if I should call the police, the doorman, run into the hallway, *something*. But that only seemed to make the noise louder, and it suddenly dawned on me that it was louder because it was *coming from inside my head*! A talk with the audiologist introduced me to the term "head noise," a reproduced sound that my brain was creating, and just knowing this seemed to quiet it down a bit.

I still get them sometimes, but they've become more benign. I'll hear crickets sometimes, whole concerts of them, smack in the middle of my New York City apartment. Or a snap, crackle, pop, reminiscent of one of my favorite childhood breakfast cereals. Though the tinnitus, of course, has persisted unabated, it's a lot easier to block out than the sound of a woman screaming bloody murder.

39

"Whisper" is a word that sounds like what it is, the kind of word that creates itself when said. Whispers connect people with a soft intimacy that is quite unlike anything else.

Little girls are always whispering to one another. At summer camp, in our cabins at night, when we were all supposed to be sleeping, we would huddle on someone's bunk bed, sneaking candy from the care packages that our parents would send us and speaking to one another in urgent whispers. We would try to suppress our giggles so that the patrolling counselors wouldn't interrupt us and make us go to sleep. We would tell ghost stories and talk about the boys we had crushes on.

We wanted to whisper all night; it was so wonderful to lie there and reveal ourselves to each other, the whispers somehow making it easier to tell things that were hard to say out loud. There would be a great chorus of whispers after taps was played over the loudspeaker, signaling bedtime, then sometimes a long, solo rising and falling as one of us recounted a tale. Late at night, much later, our soft, drowsy sentences soothed each other to sleep.

There were the wonderfully scandalous whispers of my youth, too: Bored at synagogue, a Bar Mitzvah, a school assembly, or any and all adult gatherings where we were supposed to behave, my brothers and friends and I would whisper to one another, "Is this over yet?" "This is sooo boring," "How can we sneak out?" We would whisper jokes and snide remarks, trying to make one another laugh to interrupt the silence, reveling in the tiny anarchies of our whispers. And there were the boys, my school-age sweethearts. Their lips against the lobe of my ear. Their breath, warm and damp, their sweet words just for me.

I can't remember the last whisper I heard, though it must have been more than a decade ago. I realized in college that I needed to keep my hearing aids in if I wanted to absorb the quiet compliments and pleadings and encouragements that mark the change from childhood crushes to more adult intimacy. Without my consent, without preparing for this specific loss, sweet nothings simply became nothings.

The whisper is lost to me. One of life's greatest yet most common and simple intimacies has vanished.

Most people around me know the futility of whispering to me. These days, on the rare occasion when I am whispered to by someone who has just come into my life—a new boyfriend, a fresh confidante—it is nothing but hot air being blown into my ear canal. It makes me sad, but when I see people whispering to each other, I don't begrudge them the act. I do feel a longing for what I can no longer hear, but, even more, I feel joy that for even a small piece of my life I was able to experience whispering in all its forms.

These days, I notice how quickly a whisper passes between people, how it is given and accepted and is gone. Sometimes I want to tell those people to take just a few more seconds to appreciate that whisper and its strange, gentle force. I'd like to go back and find those little girls in their cabin, on that bunk bed in the dark, and tell them to stay up tonight, to whisper to each other, whisper as long as they can.

40

Caroline and I have found our own way to whisper.

Every couple of weeks, we have a sleepover. As we lie next to each other in my bed, she'll wait for a moment while I take my hearing aids out and place them with my glasses on the nightstand. Once the lights are out we practically transform into preteen girls having a sleepover, though with me no longer able to see or hear, we are left to whisper our secrets using only our hands. At first, Caroline learned sign language from me, and then continued, for me, *for us,* and now we are both practicing our tactile sign, the language used by people who are both deaf and blind. This way, no matter how dark or noisy it is, or however limited my hearing or vision becomes, we will always be able to talk to each other.

We'll lie facing one another, and she'll take both of my hands and place hers inside of them. As her hand begins to take form, I'll start to sound out the word she is spelling in my hand, listening intently with my palm and fingers, closing my eyes to help me focus. While I hold and follow the movement of her hands, Caroline will bring her pointer finger to her chest, and I'll speak aloud what she is signing. As her pointer finger continues into its next sign, she'll wait for me to speak each word to be sure that I have understood her.

At first we were terrible at it, and I would start to giggle at every mistake—most of them mine—and though I couldn't hear Caroline, I knew she was giggling, too, because I could feel the quick little bounces her upper body would make against the bed. Like a child's game of telephone, the more confused we got, the funnier it was, and each mistake would make us laugh harder. Caroline could hear the sound of my laughter loud and clear, but she knew that I couldn't hear hers, so she would take my hand and place it against her neck right at her vocal cords, so that I could feel her laughing, which made me laugh even harder.

We've gotten better at it, and sometimes I'm astonished at what we've accomplished in the complete silence and darkness. Now I know that I will never be alone, no matter how dark and silent my world may become, and Caroline knows that she will never lose me.

Watching people tactile-sign is like watching two people embrace, an elaborate dance of hands and fingers. When people communicate through tactile sign they stand close, facing each other, their arms moving in unison and their hands acting as eyes, ears, and voices.

With Facebook and texting and everything else that has replaced face-to-face communication, even a phone call can feel like a rare intimacy these days (unless you're in my family, where no one seems able to go for more than six hours without calling one another).

Tactile sign, though, is by its very nature intimate. It requires close touch and total concentration on another person. It is the only way to communicate one-on-one without sight or hearing, and it is how Annie Sullivan famously blew open Helen Keller's prison of silence and darkness, holding her hands under the spigot and then signing "water" into them over and over, until it came alive in her hands.

Tactile sign requires time and patience, two things that seem to be in short supply these days—for me included. It is not something you can do while multitasking, half-listening while you type an email or flip through a magazine. It requires giving someone else your full attention while they give you theirs, which is, when you think about it, an extraordinarily rare thing. Your mind can't simply wander to other things—what you're going to have for lunch, the work you need to get done, the things that are constantly running through the backs of our minds while we do something else—because your total attention is needed here, in the present, in your sensitive palms and fingertips.

It also requires a level of physical intimacy that many of us are uncomfortable with. There is no masking your feelings behind a keyboard, no looking away, no distance. It is honest and generally free of small talk, and it can feel strange and a little scary to be that physically close to someone, but it is also extraordinarily exhilarating to be able to experience people in such a different and meaningful way.

This is a way that I will always be able to keep my precious relationships, and maybe even to make new ones, with those patient enough to try. I can't imagine a life that only contracts and doesn't expand to include new friends. If I am blind and deaf, will I still be able to know and love new people? A part of me is skeptical, but then I think of Helen Keller, of how much she loved others and loved the world. She accomplished so much in her life and inspired so many people, and thinking of her gives me the strength to know that I can do this, that I can have a fulfilling, joyful life no matter how much I lose.

When we watch most people with their pets or newborn babies, we can see how gently they treat them and the affection that is given so easily from one to the other. With their big eyes and total innocence, babies and dogs are so easy to love, and to touch and be touched by without fear.

One of the most important things that I have learned in my field of work is that people crave human connection and need to be touched. Those who don't like it, and who shy away from touch, generally have been given a good reason to be wary of it. In my practice I keep pillows with textures on the couch and chair in my office, and I frequently watch people recount a memory while using a fingertip to outline the bumpy stitching on one of those pillows. Others hug one to their chest as they speak to me in session. They use them for comfort, or to express fidgeting anxiety or even happiness, and I can pick up on more about them by the way that they are touching things.

I think that the importance of touch is often overlooked in everyday life, especially once we become adults. As children, we wrestle and chase and throw our arms around those we love with wholehearted affection. Study after study has shown that people who are touched more are happier and live longer, but I don't think most of us are touched nearly enough. I grew up in a houseful of huggers. We are all affectionate and snuggly and feel comfortable in one another's space. For me, touch is imperative. It grounds me and connects me to people, and it is a huge part of how I communicate. I don't want to have to live without seeing or hearing, but I can, and will, live a good life without those senses. Nobody can survive without being touched.

41

People often tell me that I'm an inspiration, for my zest and enthusiasm for life, my lack of self-pity, my acceptance of what I'm facing. I'm never sure what to say or how I feel about that. If there is anything that makes me inspirational, it's the things that people don't see or know about, the perseverance to get through the general navigations of everyday life.

Like when I've negotiated my way through the crowded sidewalks to the busy subway, and there is construction that is pounding through my hearing aids, so I take them out and read my book while I wait, *and miss the subway that is right in front of me,* because I have neither seen nor heard it, and decide to laugh about it, rather than let it get me down.

So being told I'm an inspiration can make me feel uncomfortable, except when it comes from my brother. I don't mind when Peter says that I'm his hero, because I can say, in all honesty, "No, you're *my* hero!" Peter is my number one advocate, supporter, and interpreter in dark and loud situations. He is also unquestionably the most patient, caring person I know, and hilariously funny, as well. I have always admired his extraordinary ability to meet someone with no prejudgments, and the empathy he has that allows him to put himself in someone else's shoes, look out through their eyes. It's so rare, and it's so important.

Peter is the guy you always want on your team—not always because he's the best player, but because he is its unbridled enthusiastic heart. He exudes positive energy, even when things are tough, and he has the unique ability to immediately make you feel comfortable in your own skin—to recognize and accept you for being exactly who you are. Singing and dancing with my siblings has always been a joy for me, being able to groove and goof around together, and if you're ready to have a good time, say, wholeheartedly singing your favorite cheesy love song from the '80s (preferably Debbie Gibson, in his case), Peter is your man and will join in and belt it out with you. If he doesn't know the words, he'll still sing as though he does or he'll dance enthusiastically to support your vocals.

Over the past several years, my ability to see and hear in a dark and noisy restaurant has become increasingly compromised. I often just sit quietly and get lost in my own thoughts. The background noise is simply too loud for me to hear the person speaking, and my field of vision is too narrow for me to follow the conversation as it bounces back and forth. It's not that I'm not enjoying myself; it just requires a lot of effort on my part and the patience and willingness of others to repeat what's been said. For many, even though they love me, I know it takes away from the ease and fun of their evening, and the truth is, a lot of what's been said may not be worth the effort of repeating. When Peter's there, though, I always have a good time. He's sensitive to my needs and normalizes them with humor and grace. When we are gathered at a table with friends or family at a restaurant, he'll encourage people to speak a little louder or to speak in my direction. Peter is so familiar with my sense of humor that he knows when I've actually heard what's been said and when I am faking it. People will laugh hysterically over a joke and calm down—the punch line has been delivered, the moment is over—and Peter will repeat the story for me just because he knows that I would have laughed hysterically with everyone else had I heard it the first time. And I always do, which makes him laugh, too. It's so much better to laugh with someone else.

One of the hardest things to have lost is the ability to laugh in a crowd. I can't imagine anything worse than living without laughter; it sucks to not hear the joke when everyone else does. The people closest to me are quick and witty, and laughing is just what we *do*. I want to laugh along with them, and I want to make them laugh. Luckily, it's as important to Peter and Alan and Caroline, and they'll always repeat something for me to make sure I get to. Peter is the best of all at ferrying laughter to me when it doesn't reach me the first time.

When the waiter is reciting the specials for the evening, Peter will repeat them to me quietly as I lean in to him and listen closely with my left ear. It often sounds a little something like this: "Halibut with capers, tomatoes, and olives; filet mignon prepared with potatoes, green beans, and hopefully not whatever just flew out of the waiter's mouth . . ."

One night, he took me to see Billy Crystal performing one of his shows, *700 Sundays*. When the show had started and I tried to use the assistive-listening headphones, we realized that they weren't working, so he tried to repeat everything that I missed that he knew I'd think was funny.

At one point, the entire audience was laughing hysterically, except for me. Peter could tell I had missed what had been said, because it was a fart joke, and I always laugh at those. So he repeated it for me, and as the rest of the audience quieted down, I started laughing solo and hysterically, which Billy actually heard from the stage. In the blinding stage light he looked out to the audience in my direction and said, "You like that one, huh?" This of course only made me laugh harder.

People, understandably, find it hard to joke with me about my sight and hearing loss, but I often need to laugh about it, and Peter gets that. One night, at a big, loud dinner with family and friends, a joke was told, and I couldn't hear it. My hearing aids often pick up the wrong sounds, loud background noise rather than what I'm trying to focus on. After Peter had repeated the punch line for me several times and I continued to look at him inquisitively, he finally enunciated as slowly and clearly as possible.

"*I . . . SAID . . . DID . . . YOU . . . GET . . . THE . . . JOKE . . . YOU . . . FUCKING . . . IDIOT?!*" It sent me into hysterics more than the joke ever could have, not only because he slowed down his speech to talk to me like I was an idiot but also because he sounded like such a "fucking idiot" himself speaking to me that way, parroting the way that people sometimes speak to the hearing impaired, as though they are mentally impaired as well.

This is now a running joke between us, and one that has been picked up by others close to me. If I don't hear him after a couple of times, he'll come out with something like, "What . . . are . . . you . . . going . . . to . . . eat . . . tonight . . . fuck-er?"

If I have to go blind and deaf, I'm glad I can have a sense of humor about it. I don't mind being teased, and sometimes the things I mishear can be hilarious. Caroline and I were having lunch with a friend one day, and he asked if either one of us had ever gotten toe fungus from showering at the gym, to which I responded, "Yeah! I had it on my bagel this morning." I had heard "tofu cream cheese." We couldn't stop laughing.

42

There are so many beautiful places in the world that I've been lucky enough to see, and so many more that I long to. I know I won't have enough time to see nearly as much of the world as I want to, so I hold these memories close, the way I try to do with all of my experiences that are gone or won't last.

After I graduated from college I went to Europe for a month. Armed with a Eurail pass, a *Let's Go Europe,* and a far-too-overstuffed backpack—items that anyone who has taken this journey is intimately familiar with—I flew to Italy to meet my friend Andy. Our plan was to meet up in Florence, and travel to Greece and Sicily and wherever the wind blew us.

Like countless others before me, I fell instantly in love with the city, the narrow, cobblestone streets—hazardous though they were for me—and the little shops tucked into them. I loved the sexy, robust sound of people speaking Italian, and the rumble of Vespas whipping by, which would have me jumping back onto the curb just as a handsome man would ride by, almost always accompanied by a stylish woman on the back. Everything was bathed in an incandescent pink light, making the people even more beautiful, and at the market I bought half a dozen silk scarves in a riot of jewel tones. The colors, tastes, and smells all felt more vibrant. And the food! I would have bathed in the olive oil if they'd let me. I ate gelato, sometimes twice a day. I couldn't believe how impossibly fresh everything tasted. I had always been a picky eater, but apparently food in Italy had become the exception. Even the strong scent of the Italian men's cologne, which normally would have repulsed me, smelled right here.

From there we took a boat to Greece and flew to the tiny, beautiful islands of Santorini, Mykonos, Ios, and Paros. The islands were stunning—the azure water against the white stone with the stores and restaurants literally carved into the rock—and I knew these images would stay etched in my memory forever.

I met up with another friend a week later, and we flew to France. I loved the timeless character of the old buildings in Paris, the sophistication of the people, and the ease with which you could walk through the city. We traipsed from the tiny, vibrant Marais to the splendor of the Tuileries Garden, walked along the Seine, and roamed the halls of the Louvre. And we ate, savoring the incredible food, the incomparable cheeses and breads and pastries.

From there we traveled to Germany and visited Dachau, light-years away from the joy of Italy, the beauty of Paris, and the pure white sunshine of Greece. The day we went was appropriately gray and rainy, and freezing. As we walked into a large and bitterly cold building that was the gas chamber, I was filled with the horror and sadness of all of the people—mothers and fathers and sisters and brothers—who had been forced to die in there. It felt poisoned, as did the earth around us that held the mass graves of so many dead.

It was as awful and heartbreaking as I expected it to be. I'm so glad, though, that I got to see it, to experience a place that I needed my eyes for. I will never let myself forget what I saw there.

. . . .

My mom and I went to Peru for her sixtieth birthday, when I was twenty-eight. It was a walking and hiking tour, and I wanted to do the most intense hikes. My mom got terrible blisters and stayed toward the back for much of it, whereas I, of course, wanted to lead the pack and push myself to my absolute limit. More than wanted to; I felt like I needed to. There is nothing I love more than hiking, because it makes me feel so able, so focused, so capable of taking care of myself. There are ways in which we are all weak and in which we are all strong. This is one of my strengths, and even though my foot and back ached, as they always do, it was an ache that I could handle, could push through, and it didn't stop me from loving the feeling of being in my own flawed, strong body.

For the bravest (or craziest) among us, there was the Inca Trail, which winds its way around the back of Machu Picchu to the Gate of the Sun. Parts of it are so steep that you need to crawl to climb it, and there are ancient, narrow steps leading to the summit. I was determined to climb it, and I knew that I could. When I am completely focused on my body, I can forget my eyes and ears and just concentrate on the parts of my body that work as well as everyone else's. Also, my central vision was still very strong, and as narrow as it was I could totally focus on what was directly in front of me. In fact, it probably helped me, because my lack of peripheral vision made it easy to block out the deadly fall that you could take on either side. I was so exhilarated, and my mom was at the top, cheering for me. When we reached the peak

I could barely speak, sweat pouring down my face. I felt like I had conquered the world.

My eyes swept over the scene in front of me, scanning from side to side to take in all of the beauty. The mist hung over the wide swaths of green and the massive ruins. I kept thinking, *I am seeing this. I will never forget this.* I was just so amazed; I wanted to be able to take in everything, to fill my eyes with all the beauty and wonder of the world. For everyone, it was a breathtaking sight, and the cameras came out, capturing that unbelievable vista. For me, though, I was less intent on getting a great photo and more focused on using all of my senses to take it all in. In addition to the beauty all around me, there was my pounding heart, the breeze drying my sweat, the smell of the high mountain air. So I did what I always try to do: close my eyes and capture the feeling, the moment, the memory, to bring back when it's not here anymore. This was an extraordinary, once-in-a-lifetime trip, but I try to remember to do the same thing with simpler, everyday moments: imprint them on my memory and let myself feel the full joy of being there in that moment.

After we left Machu Picchu we made our way through little Incan villages, past tiny huts with a fire burning in the center of them, watching the villagers in their colorful clothes and the children watching us shyly or chasing after one another. It was so peaceful and quiet, and the people made do with so little. I wanted to be able to make do with this little, and at that moment I liked to believe that I could.

When Mom and I got to the little cabins where we were sleeping that night, I started crying, and Mom hugged me. Peter and I both cry when we're overwhelmed with happiness, and I stood in our cabin, tears pouring down my face as Mom held me, feeling so happy and strong and so fortunate to have all that I did.

Polly, Lauren, and I are planning a trip to climb Mount Kilimanjaro next year, a trip Polly promised me we would take someday when I was twelve. This would make me nervous, except that I'll be with two of the toughest women in my life. Lauren, now twenty, is an incredible athlete who was once on the Olympic development team for soccer, and the fiercest advocate I could ask for. Once after taking my spin class she overheard a woman complain that she had tried to get my attention in the middle of class and I had ignored her, and Lauren was over there in a flash, explaining my condition and letting her know, in no uncertain terms, that if she needed my help all she had to do was ask. She knows that there is nothing that I hate more than being misunderstood and that I want everyone in my classes to feel comfortable and accommodated. I have no doubt that if I am hiking between Lauren and Polly, I can make it to the top of Kilimanjaro.

43

Every year on February 4, which is Daniel's and my birthday, I always make sure that I think of a wish just in the moment when people are singing "Happy Birthday," so that I have it ready as I blow the candles out. When we were younger, I remember wishing that I would get a Cabbage Patch Kid, and after Mom and Dad separated, I'd wish that they would get back together. In high school I wished that Cody and I would get married and be together forever. For the last twelve years I have had the same wish: Right before I blow out the candles, I always say to myself, "I wish that Danny will get better," or "I wish that Danny will be able to live the life he wants." It doesn't seem to be working so far, and I've tried to think of another wish, but you only get one and I don't want to waste it; this is the one thing that I want most in the world, and just in case wishing for it helps, I make sure that I do.

Daniel tried different medications and therapies for years, but none of them worked the way he needed them to: no matter what it was or how much he took. He tried everything, from the most benign to the most severe and drastic therapies available, but to no avail. As with me, it seemed there was no cure, nothing that could help him. My heart broke over and over for him.

He practiced yoga incessantly, meditated, had acupuncture treatments. He wanted to get better. Dan was the smartest person I knew, and I couldn't imagine how it must feel, in his more lucid moments, to know that his mind was not in his control. He seesawed from wildly enthusiastic and ebullient to devastatingly depressed. Then he decided that he was going to take a trip to Peru to go on a spirit walk in the Amazon to participate in a tribal ceremony led by a Shaman, where he would drink ayahuasca, a strong hallucinogen brewed from Amazonian plant leaves that has been used for centuries by the natives for healing purposes. Danny was determined to do this, and when we realized that we couldn't talk him out of it, my father decided to go with him.

As hard as it was for me to accept this alternative "therapy," I understood Danny's compulsion to find something that would help him. In my case, people are constantly telling me about new therapies, treatments, and natural remedies that might help me, but I'm generally skeptical. When something truly viable comes along, I'll hear about it. When Daniel made the decision to go to Peru, my gut said, *This cannot possibly be good for someone in as fragile a state as Danny,* but at that point all I could do was support him.

At first, the emails that came in were positive, and I began to think that maybe he would be okay. I imagined that he was discovering a new culture and people, and I hoped that perhaps getting away from his own small world for a while would help him. Then came my father's email after the first ayahuasca ceremony. It had gone well, and my dad said that he had felt like he was with the "old Dan."

During the last ceremony, though, Daniel had collapsed into

four hours of sobbing and thrashing . Despite this, Danny still believed that the ayahuasca was helping him let go of his demons, and that if he could stay longer and take more he would start to heal. It was agonizing to think of Daniel going through so much pain and anguish in the hopes of healing himself. My dad continued the email by telling us that Daniel was now terrified to be left alone for even a minute, and reminded us that we should not be expecting to see the "old Dan."

This is an expression that my family used for a long time. "The old Dan." We all used it, but I finally realized that we had to stop saying it, because it let us believe that he might get back to the person he once was. He's not going back to his former self any more than I am, though there is a big difference: While my hearing and vision are vastly diminished, they are not the essential parts of who I am. For Daniel to have his beautiful brain not in his control is a much more horrifying thought.

After I got my father's email, I immediately booked a ticket to San Francisco, finding a flight that landed only an hour after they would arrive from Peru, knowing that I needed to be there. As soon as I saw him and hugged him, I could tell that he was far from okay. He had a terrified look in his eyes, and he couldn't stop moving, his body vibrating in my arms. For the week that I was there, I tried not to leave his side, and I slept next to him in the guesthouse, the very place I had lived while I recovered from my accident years earlier. He held on to me like I was a life raft, only able to sleep for an hour or less at a time. I kept my hearing aids in so that I could hear him when he cried out. My incredible, intense brother. My precious Danny. My twin, whom I would do anything to protect, who would do anything to protect me, though we are both helpless in the face of each other's conditions.

Someone sent me a video recently of twins being born in a water birth. When they are first born, they are held, suspended in the water, and have not yet opened their eyes and become aware of their surroundings, so they are still behaving as they did in the womb. They curl around one another, bodies intertwining, snuggling, pushing, one entity that has never known being without the other. Daniel and I have this connection, and I can't help thinking that I'm the one who should be able to help him most. We clung to each other for nine months. He was my first love, our bodies holding each other in whatever dreamlike state we dwelled in before birth, and there is something about that connection that is impenetrable. When Danny and I are home at the same time we often still share a bed. It is so natural for us, and I've always thought it was because we had that time together, before there was anyone else. It makes me feel so secure and peaceful, knowing that we are safe lying next to each other.

. . . .

More than anything else, living with a disability is exhausting. It can be hugely lonely to be different. My disease is particularly isolating, and so is my brother's. The irony of all of this is that he keeps my parents from worrying too much about me. Is Daniel any more able to change than I am? People seem to draw stark distinctions between physical and mental disabilities, when they are so murky.

Daniel and I are equally desperate to help each other and we are both filled with survivor's guilt. I know that most of the time he doesn't understand that he is far more debilitated than I am, and I wouldn't trade places with him for a second. He is desperate to help me and calls to apologize, to tell me his next plan to make money so that he can get me a car and a driver, take care of me, make sure that I have everything that I need.

There are ways in which Daniel's and my circumstances are quite similar, except that I am applauded for living my life to the best of my ability, while his situation is thought of as tragically sad and has put immense emotional and financial strain on my family, which he is aware enough of to feel badly about. I was lucky to have some information at a relatively young age about what my future would hold, so that I could begin to prepare myself for what lay ahead. My parents exposed me to blindness and a supportive community, I was taught how to advocate for myself at school and in life to get the things I needed, and I learned the skills I needed to help myself as much as I could as my hearing and vision got worse. I was responsible for making the doctor appointments, going to the audiologist, and getting all of the training that I needed. I decided to learn sign language and integrate myself into the deaf community.

Daniel was never taught these same skills. When we were growing up, Daniel was exceptional at everything, effortlessly, and was never a show-off or arrogant about anything. He didn't need to be. So I can't imagine how devastating it must have been for him when, years later, he was suddenly confronted with losing all of that to a disease that he had no understanding of. Great things were expected of him and he knew that nobody was surprised by his successes, whereas my every accomplishment was thought off as beating the odds.

Daniel needed serious help. In contrast to the welcoming disability services programs that had embraced me with open arms, Dan had a very different experience. After trying dozens of different medications from numerous doctors, all of which had terrible side effects, or didn't do the job they were meant to,

Danny became distrustful of anything that was offered to him. Unlike what I had experienced with my own disabilities, when Daniel became ill there was no welcoming disability services program there to embrace him with open arms. Mental illness distorts your view of the world, but it also alters how the world sees you. When we see a person with a physical disability we often offer to help, feel pity, or maybe feel inspired to appreciate what we have and what we're able to do. When most of us see a person who is clearly mentally ill, though, our immediate reaction is to avoid him, increasing those feelings of isolation even more.

I think that Daniel's road is much harder than mine, because his brilliant mind struggles every day to recapture the clarity and sharpness that always came so naturally to him. He feels betrayed by his own brain, and lives with constant fear and anxiety about the future. Although I am losing my sight and hearing, I can still have a joyful, meaningful life. I can face what's coming to me, and my network of support helps and grounds me. Danny is rootless and completely disabled in so many ways.

It's impossible not to be keenly aware of the irony between my situation and Daniel's, and sometimes I get frustrated when he can't even appreciate how fortunate he is to be inside his beautifully able body, with its perfect eyes and ears. Even I can fall into this trap, of somehow treating mental illness as though it were any less real, any less physical, than mine. It's not.

He now lives mostly in his car, in San Diego. It is the fourth car that he has had, since he rarely leaves it, and has spent much of the last several years driving endlessly from San Diego to Los Angeles and back again. He calls me daily, full of grandiose ideas, talking in circles that lead to nowhere. It doesn't matter how bad my hearing is anymore, how fast he talks, or whether he mumbles, because he always tells me the same things and talks about the same plans he never follows through with. He talks endlessly about his desire to make a fortune so that he can always take care of me. And then, in his lowest moments, he tells me that the only reason he hasn't taken his own life is because he knows how much his family loves him. I am so scared that at some point, as my Usher progresses, I won't be able to be there enough for him. Daniel dodged my genetic bullet, but I dodged a bigger one. I'm not the one that my parents' hearts break over. I'm the lucky one. When Danny calls I may feel exasperated, sad, and guilty, but I always feel the deep, intense connection to the first person I ever loved.

44

I'd been told for many years that this day would come, and though a part of me had never really believed it, here it was: the dreaded cane. The thing that announces to the world, "Look at me! I'm blind!" People don't notice the spectrum of seeing disabilities. You have a cane, ergo, you must be blind. I'm sure that I would have thought the same thing, if I hadn't been all too aware of the degrees of blindness.

Several years before, when I had gone out to practice alone for the first time, a part of me had been very curious, but mostly I had just been filled with dread. After a deep breath I had stepped out onto the sidewalk, scanning quickly for others on the block. It was already dark out, and, for the moment, I had been alone on the street. Slowly, I unfolded the cane and it snapped right into shape. Click, click, click, click. As quickly as a tape measure retreats to its dispenser. Its tip was a reflective, fluorescent red, and if there was any reason for a stranger to question my walking slowly back and forth from my apartment building to the end of the street, this would clear things right up.

It wasn't so bad at first. I held it down low so that I wouldn't see it. I hadn't practiced since I had received training years before, and I tried to remember what I had learned. Two-point touch. Tap left, tap right, tap left, tap right . . . constant contact, side to side, shorelining, overlap, protective technique, upper forearm, lower forearm, all of the things that I had been taught. Things that I probably should have listened more closely to. I had integrated myself into the deaf community, loving sign and the ease with which I could use it, but I hadn't worked as hard when it came to my vision. Not even close.

When I finally decided that I really needed to start learning to use the cane, I had a mobility trainer named Nicole, a loud, proud, outspoken lesbian who was quick to provide commentary on, or criticism of, anyone in our way. We would go out on the street to practice, and, as if I didn't already feel like I was drawing enough attention to myself, I had a woman with no care for social graces or patience loudly ordering directions at me. Despite this, or maybe even because of it, I adored her. It takes a little while to understand blind culture; it has its own qualities, just like the deaf community. There is an enormous amount of animation in the voice, the way, in the deaf culture, facial features and gestures look overexaggerated. To sighted people, the voices of the blind can seem socially awkward sometimes, but when you can't see, all of the information you are conveying comes from your voice. I think visually impaired people can also seem extra touchy to others, but it's because touch is vital for someone who can't see. Your fingertips are your eyes; laying your hand on someone's arm is a way of smiling at them, even if you can't look into their eyes or they can't see yours.

Nicole was patient with me. I knew I probably wasn't easy to teach, because I was so focused on the cane that it became harder to concentrate on my hearing, and I had to work not to let my mind wander. She understood that my difficulties were twofold, though, and she gave me her all, and I'm sure she cut me what she would consider some slack.

When Nicole left she told me that I should be practicing with the cane every day, and when she called a couple of weeks later to find out how it was going, I was indeed using the cane. It had turned out to be an ideal tool for grabbing Olive's toys without having to leave the couch. She asked if I'd been practicing regularly, and, as I picked up Sophie the squeaky giraffe for the thirtieth time that morning, I assured her that it was getting lots of use.

That first night when I had gone out to try my cane in the dark, I had gathered everything I remembered and turned my full attention to the task at hand. I approached the crosswalk at the end of the block, and a car halted at the stop sign and waited. I stayed at the corner, willing him to drive by so that I could go slowly, drawing as little attention to myself as possible. He stayed there, waiting for me to cross. Finally I did, and as I entered the crosswalk I suddenly felt an overwhelming need to cry. I could see the driver scrutinizing me, and though I had wanted this to feel freeing, knowing that I would learn to be independent by doing it, I hated being watched. By the time I was across the street tears were streaming down my face, and then I *really* couldn't see. As soon as the car was gone I immediately crossed back over and retreated back into my apartment, sobbing. I hated it, and I hated knowing that at some point in the not too distant future I would be doing this for the rest of my life.

Now, years later, the day had come when I needed it for real. The night, actually, that was when I really needed it. I reminded myself that I could still do things myself during the day, and, as hard as they were getting, I told myself that I was lucky. I was thirty years old, and the doctors had thought I would be completely blind by now. It didn't help. This was worse than the hearing aids I was supposed to start wearing in high school, which I would take out unless I absolutely needed them, or cover under my long hair, still able then to keep my disabilities hidden away. This cane was the opposite of hidden away. It was like a giant banner hanging over me.

I stood on the curb and wished for Caroline, or Peter, or my mom, *someone* to take my arm, to be with me as I did this. I reminded myself that this is for when they're not here, so that I can do things for myself, go places by myself, keep my precious independence. That wasn't helping, either. So again, I took a deep breath and stepped out onto the sidewalk, clicking the cane into place, remembering all of the challenges I had faced between that first trial run and now. I had hoped that it would be easier this time, that what I had learned, experienced, gained, and lost in those years would help me to be able to face this with more acceptance. It didn't. This time, though, I had no choice but to walk forward, in the present, into my future. I straightened my back, tried to swallow my tears, and took a step, and then another, making my way down the sidewalk.

45

A few years ago, I went home with Caroline for Christmas at
her parents' house in East Hampton. I couldn't wait. I adore
Caroline's parents, and they've become such a huge part of my
life and so close to my family. Peter actually calls Caroline's mom
on Mother's Day.

Christmas is a huge deal for them, and I had heard endlessly
from Caroline about the wonder that was the holiday season at
the Kaczors'. Every year their tree goes up the day after Thanksgiving, and after that it is open season on the Christmas insanity.
Caroline had told me all about the Christmas extravaganza, so I
thought I knew what to expect, but I couldn't have imagined the
winter wonderland (her words) that awaited us. She was psyched
to share the Christmas magic (again, her words) with me. A couple of days before Christmas she picked me up at the Helen Keller
National Center, after I had had a day of grueling back-to-back
appointments with an audiologist, an optometrist, a mobility
trainer, and a computer technology accessibility instructor, all of
whom, for whatever reason, had been in shitty moods. The

holidays seem to delight some people and leave others glowering. Caroline is definitely in the former category, and as soon as I got into the car her joy and excitement quickly cheered me up as she put on the special Christmas CD she had burned just for the trip, singing along in a mocking, playful way. I started to sing, too, but five minutes into the drive my hearing aids were out and I was sound asleep, out of sheer exhaustion from a day of testing and learning the ropes for functioning as a deaf/blind person. By the time I woke up we were only a few blocks away from Caroline's house, and she was almost jumping out of her seat with excitement.

As we drove up to the house, I suddenly understood what all the fuss was about. Oh sweet baby Jesus, it was something to behold. A set of three snowmen awaited us on the front steps, and when we got close they began singing and dancing. Their sensors, apparently, were so sensitive that anything from a car driving by to a raccoon racing across the yard could set them off. I was the only one in the house who wouldn't be woken up at one point or another by the sound of singing snowmen in the middle of the night.

Caroline's father, Larry, was in charge of the outdoor decorations. White lights, tinsel, and red bows were wrapped around the deck, and a fourth sensored snowman, two-feet tall and stuffed, stood by the door greeting everyone who came in. "Come on in, it's warm inside!" Tommy the snowman would cheer. He also did this when people left, or stood on the porch, or got anywhere near him. It was one of those times that I was aware of the advantages of having ears that I could turn off.

Her mom, Susanne, handled the indoor affairs: the splendid tree, Christmas music, snow globes, and stockings. The decorated hearth and cozy fires, the scented peppermint soap and Christmas towels in the bathroom. There were gingerbread men and

Santa's entire family hanging on every possible nail, hook, and banister. I couldn't help but love it. And there was banana bread, my favorite, baked especially for me. Caroline gave me her bedroom and took the guest room, because hers was closer to the bathroom, and I wouldn't have to pass by a steep set of stairs to get there.

They made me feel so welcome in their little winter wonderland, which had always been built just for three, that I wanted to help as much as I could and make them happy that they had invited me. The three of them have always been a tight unit. Caroline is an only child who's extraordinarily close to both of her parents, and, even though I probably shouldn't have, even though Caroline was my best friend, I still felt like I needed to earn my place there. Lucky Rebecca, to have wonderful Caroline to help her, to find her lost things, sign to her in loud rooms, help her find her way in the dark, bring her home to share and celebrate her favorite holiday, and even give up her bedroom for her.

So after every meal I would jump up to clear the table and help clean the kitchen. On Christmas day I broke a bowl and felt terrible about it, though everyone had assured me it wasn't a big deal at all. So I was exceedingly careful after Christmas dinner when Caroline's mom handed me a large platter to dry. I still managed to drop it; it slipped out of my hand and shattered to pieces on the floor, so loudly that hearing the full force of it threw me back in shock. I froze, and then, like a terribly guilty and clumsy child, ran to the bathroom and started to cry. I felt completely absurd, but I couldn't stop. Did they really want me here? Did they just feel sorry for me? A bowl *and* a platter? Really, Beck? Probably heirlooms, passed down carefully from generation to generation, used especially for the Christmas feast. Which I had ruined.

Susanne followed me and stood so close to me that I could barely see her face. She knew that, though, and was doing it to make sure I heard every word that she said. "Becky," she told me, using my family nickname, the one that my parents use, "you must know that you are more precious to us than all the china in our cabinets." I tried to stop crying, to stop acting like a child, to believe this kind, generous woman who I knew meant it. What I really wanted to do, though, was sob in her arms, to ask why it was always me needing help, why I couldn't be the helper. It was all I had ever wanted to do. It made me so happy to help. Instead I just stood there, nodding, wanting to reassure her, not wanting her to feel bad about something I'd done. Twice. In one day.

. . . .

My gratitude to the universe for bringing Caroline and me together is unending. What I can sometimes forget is that she feels as grateful as I do. So once when Susanne saw me thanking Caroline, for what was probably the umpteenth time that day, for helping me find something, she came over and sat with me, putting her hands on mine, again keeping her face close to mine, so that I could hear every word. In her firm yet calm second-grade-teacher voice, she told me how much I had changed Caroline's life.

She told me that before Caroline had met me, she had been so unsure of herself and what she wanted to do with her life, and had kept herself walled off from the world. That getting to know me helped her have the confidence to become a spin instructor, and that my encouragement is what made her brave enough to apply to graduate school. She is now a social worker, which is a job that fits her perfectly, because she, too, loves to help people.

Caroline and her mom told me that I brought her back into the world. They told me a story about a day when Caroline's father had come home, jubilant, after dropping her off at the jitney to return to the city after a spin training course she'd attended out in the Hamptons. Usually Caroline stayed slouched in his car until the bus arrived, and then, at the very last minute, dodged to it alone. After we met one another, though, and they drove up, she saw me waiting there and eagerly got out, telling him she was fine and that he could leave. Caroline walked up to me and we talked for the whole ride back to the city. Such a small thing, but so enormous and triumphant to her parents.

I had trouble imagining the Caroline that they were describing. Though I knew these things about her—the depression, the eating disorder, the need to be alone—it was so hard to connect them to my hysterically funny, outgoing, driven best friend. Knowing that I was a part of that change, and that while my help didn't show in the way hers did, in all of those small everyday things, it was there, made all the difference, as did hearing the words that her mother said. "Caroline helps you, yes, but you have given her the confidence to overcome obstacles and take on challenges she may never have taken on. Her father and I are forever grateful to you. Never underestimate the good you do."

I can't begin to describe how much those words meant to me. Being acknowledged and appreciated, for all of us, is an essential part of living a life that we feel good about because we are reminded that we matter.

Just saying to someone, "Thanks for being such a good mom" or "You're a wonderful friend" can mean so much to people. So I forgot about the platter and just basked in the love of this wonderful family, who had become a part of my family.

But I stayed away from the china cabinet.

46

When I was twelve, the ophthalmologist told my parents that I would need a guide dog by the time I was twenty. I don't have a guide dog. I have Olive.

Guide dogs are extremely well-trained animals, carefully chosen after rigorous discipline and testing. I picked Olive because she was the cutest thing I'd ever seen, and if not for Caroline I doubt she'd be housebroken. Guide dogs are also extraordinarily smart and obedient. Olive is very smart, though I think "wily" might be a more apt description.

. . . .

I had gone to California in December of 2010, and Polly had offered to buy me a puppy for the holidays. I was beside myself with excitement. We're all dog people in my family, and I grew up with a string of golden retrievers: Brandy, Cubbie, Star, Renner. I can remember each of their individual smells and the differences in their eyes, their head size, and their gaits. They all had distinct personalities and quirks—Cubbie had always been my favorite; not the sharpest, but the most kind and gentle dog I have ever known—and they all shared that perfect dogginess, the pure, clear heart of an animal that just wants to love and be loved. I missed that unconditional, impossibly faithful love. A dog doesn't care if you're blind, deaf, unattractive, limbless. They just want to love you and be loved in return.

Even with my wonderful friends and my growing practice, my spin classes and dates, I was lonely. And as I felt my disabilities worsening a new kind of nervousness had crept in. I didn't like coming home to an empty apartment, but I relished my independence and didn't want a roommate. A dog was the answer. A perfect, well-trained puppy, my constant companion who would play when I wanted to play, always be by my side, and only bark if there was a stranger approaching or imminent danger.

I already knew exactly what dog I wanted. A few months earlier, I had been walking home from teaching a spin class one afternoon when I saw a woman with two young children, one of whom was holding a leash. I am one of those annoying people who stops to admire every dog, petting and riling them up when I'm sure their owners just want to get moving, but when I looked down and saw this dog, I couldn't believe it. He looked just like a teddy bear. I grinned at them and they smiled back, and I thought about that dog for about four blocks and then finally said, "I've gotta have that dog!" So I turned around and raced back to retrace my steps as fast as I could. When I found them, I breathlessly apologized for stalking them and asked where they had gotten their impossibly cute dog. While the mother told me about the miniature-goldendoodle breeder in Indiana, Teddy— how could his name have been anything else?—greeted me with exactly the type of enthusiasm I hoped he would. I raced home and spent an hour on the breeder's website fawning over all of the pictures and carefully reading all of the information they provided about the breed.

This was before New York was crawling with doodles of every kind, so I really knew nothing about them, but I soon learned that they were well behaved, they didn't shed, and that the mix of the two breeds—half golden retriever, half miniature poodle— was what made their adorably shaggy hair. They reminded me of the Fraggles from *Fraggle Rock,* and I knew that this was the dog for me.

When I decided to get Olive, pretty much everyone told me it was a bad idea. Why didn't I just get a guide dog? When I told them I didn't qualify yet, they asked what I would do if I had to get one while I still had Olive. My answer was one I gave, and continue to give, over and over: "I'll cross that bridge when I get there." Wouldn't it be too much for me? How would I train her? Walk her at night? I didn't care. I was going to make it work.

Caroline and I knew that this was going to be our dog. Well, I knew. At first Caroline had resisted getting a puppy, thinking that it would just be too much work with our busy schedules, and, I'm sure, suspicious of who was going to end up doing the heavy lifting. I assured her that this was not true, and as we schlepped home a doggie playpen, bed, crate, and just about anything else a puppy could ever need or want, I could tell even through her raised eyebrows and occasional eye rolls, as I squealed over yet another adorable little squeaky toy, that she was excited.

When the day finally came to pick Olive up at the airport, there was an epic snowstorm. I was so excited that I could barely sit still in my seat as my friend Jon and I drove to the airport. "Beck, calm down," he told me, straining to see the road through the storm as I hopped up and down in my seat, asking when we'd be there, behaving alternately like an annoying child and a woman who was about to have her first baby.

I was desperate to get to her. She was only eight weeks old, and I knew that she had been held for an extended layover because of the storm. By the time her flight landed, she had been crated on the airplane for twelve hours. The instant we got to the airport I jumped out of the car, the wind so strong it slammed the car door shut behind me as I squinted to see the signs through the snow. When we got to the cargo center we saw other people standing in front of a large door, waiting for their dogs, and, even across the large room, I could hear clearly the ceaseless, high-pitched cry of one of the puppies. Somehow I knew that one must be mine. I turned and looked at Jon and he nodded. He knew it, too.

When they finally opened the doors, I rushed in, following the sound of crying; quickly found her crate; and bent down to look at her. A tiny golden ball of fur, yelping her face off. I opened the crate and she raced into my arms, licking my face, so happy to be out of her prison and held, little enough that she fit perfectly in my cupped hands. She was covered with pee and poop, and bits of shredded paper from the crate were stuck all over her. She was like a really stinky, squirming, half-finished papier-mâché project. She was absolutely perfect. My little love nugget. Up until that moment I hadn't decided on her name, but as soon as I saw her I knew she was Olive. Full name: Olivia Taco Alexander. Forever nickname: Monkey.

We wrapped her in a towel and rushed her back to the car, and I held the reeking bundle under my parka, pressed closed to me as we walked through the bitter wind and snow. I had brought Cheerios for the car ride home, and she wolfed them down, straight from my hand, eating the entire bag as the heater blew on her, warming her tiny body as it sent her funk wafting through the car. Normally the smell would have had me gagging, but something maternal had kicked in, the same way that parents have no problem changing their own children's diapers while the smell of other kids' poop revolts them.

When we got home Caroline was eagerly waiting for our return and held out her arms as soon as we walked through the door to receive our girl. I was all for playing with Olive, but Caroline, of course, insisted after one look at her that we immediately give her a bath. We were not going to have a filthy baby. After we put our bathing suits on, I stepped into the bathtub as Caroline held Olive over the side of the tub in her cupped hands. It was clear that Olive had never seen water like this before and the look of uncertainty and fear in her baby-brown eyes made me love her even more. After Caroline had cleaned her and swaddled her in towels, Olive promptly fell asleep in her arms. Three hours later Caroline was still holding her, staring in wonder down at her perfect monkey face, a darling bundle of golden curls, and I knew I had a walker, trainer, and auntie for life.

I tried to train Olive from the start, really I did. I would put her on a chair next to my bed in her crate with a little towel over it, and I would take out my hearing aids so I couldn't hear her. But I was dating a guy who would hear her crying and take her out to play. Olive was a quick study and learned right away that her loud yip would get her what she wanted. Not a great start.

Over the next few weeks she was impossible. She chewed and pulled on everything, and I had little cuts all over my hands from all of her nipping. We tried to be sure that she was never left alone in a room, but still she tore through my apartment, leaving everything in her wake in tatters.

My disabilities definitely didn't help with the training. I often didn't notice an accident until I smelled it—or stepped in it. I would stumble over mauled shoes and chewed-up eyeglasses and not notice a mangled part of the rug until my toe got snared in it. Anything I had left on a low surface was gnawed raw by her sharp puppy teeth, and within days my house was a total disaster.

With the gift of Olive, thankfully, Polly had included puppy kindergarten. We were in a class of twelve, though, so with the echo of all of the puppies and their encouraging owners in the large indoor space, I couldn't hear a thing the instructor said. Caroline was my eyes and ears, but it all moved too fast for her to sign. Despite this, in class Olive was perfect, the example of the group, proudly displaying her good behavior. The teacher, who had noticed Caroline signing to me, stopped to talk and told us that she was legally blind. When I told her that, in addition to being hearing impaired, I was also losing my vision, the look on her face and the question in her eyes was obvious without her having to say it. Why hadn't I just gotten a guide dog?

Olive's good behavior, however, was saved for class only, when she had an audience to show off for and consistently firm guidance. At home, she was an unstoppable terror with seemingly boundless energy, and, I admit, spoiled rotten. And, of course, she graduated quickly from the crate to sleeping in the bed with me. I know that there are mommy wars about this: to co-sleep or to sleep train. Olive and I are co-sleepers. My little monkey may be naughty during the day, but she is a dream to sleep with. The softest, warmest, most cuddly teddy bear imaginable.

She is also the perfect alarm clock for someone who can't see or hear one and who is chronically late. I no longer wake up in a panic, late because my vibrating alarm clock has fallen out of the bed from underneath my pillow, *again,* jumping out and inevitably smashing myself on something as I try to figure out how screwed I am for time. I am no longer racing around like an idiot, throwing my sparkly aqua retainers in the bathroom sink while simultaneously pulling on mismatched shoes and calling the gym to tell them I'm going to be a little late for my class, *again*. No, now I am awoken hours earlier than I need or would like to be. I have invested in the trustiest and most persistent alarm clock of all time.

First, there is the approach: If we have moved away from one another sometime in the night, here come Monkey's little paws, figuring out which side of me is most accessible. Then the spoon: She smushes herself into me, her back to my front, as she squirms until I wrap my arm around her and rub and scratch her belly. When I drift off again, I am quickly reminded of my duties with a distinct paw scratch across my arm. The final move, when she has decided it is time to get up: the tongue, warm, wet, and rough. First it makes its way along the circumference of my face, then up and down until I have been completely exfoliated. If this still isn't enough she often finishes off with the pièce de résistance: the monster wet willy, her tongue reaching enthusiastically into my ear. It is a move that has never failed to send me jumping out of the bed. I'm really not sure who has trained whom more, but I have my suspicions.

Olive is possessive of her place in the bed, too. If Caroline or my mom is sleeping over she'll sleep between us. Or on top of us. If there is someone else sleeping over she'll always press herself against my other side and often climb on top of me. Once when a guy I was dating was over and we were fooling around, she came over and sat on him, making it clear that she was, indeed, top dog.

It is amazing how quickly she learned to adapt to my differences. With Caroline, Olive whimpers if she wants her to get up and walk her, but with me she scratches, knowing that I won't hear a thing. She jumps out of my way if she's in a spot where I could trip on her, and walks behind me in the apartment to stay out of harm's way. If she has a toy that's in another room or stuck underneath something, she'll bark incessantly, and if I don't come in she'll stand and stare at me, bark, run to where it is, and repeat, for as long as it takes, the whines getting louder and more grating. With me, she always wins. With one stern look from Caroline she skulks off and curls up to pout.

So no, she is not a guide dog. She has chewed, to date, thousands of dollars' worth of hearing aids. She has ripped up rugs, furniture, and anything else she can get her little paws on. She knows how to walk carefully beside me, and how to behave perfectly on the subway and in public, but she will never be that patient, quiet Lab, standing sentry on the corner, waiting to help a blind owner to cross the street. She is, however, the best present that I have ever gotten and the love of my life.

If I had waited, put off getting a puppy until I needed a guide dog, or listened to the people who told me that it was just too much work, then I would have missed all of this time with my wonderful little girl. She has brought me so much laughter and happiness in the last three years. She is my companion, my baby. We should never put off what we really, really want in life. I know that I can't; I can feel time ticking away, marked by my diminished vision and hearing, and counterbalancing that with joy is integral to my life. Both personally and professionally, I have seen so many people waiting for the "perfect time" to do something that they want so badly—have a baby, switch jobs, leave a relationship—but the time is now. Why wait for the right time to pursue fulfillment and happiness? Go find it now.

And a note to my future husband, wherever you are: I'm not a big fan of candlelit dinners anymore. But if you propose to me on a sunny day in a field full of puppies, I'm all yours.

47

Most people have a favorite song, favorite food, favorite book, yes. Favorite sound, though? Probably not.

I love the sound of water. There are so many ways that we experience it. I love the sound of water running through a creek and how deep the sound of jumping into a body of water is. The changing sounds of the ebbing and flowing of the ocean's tide throughout the day, gentle and calm in the early morning as the sun comes up, charging with strength in the afternoon, then lazy and weary in the evening as the sun goes down. I love the sound of a baby happily splashing in water, and how it gurgles out of a faucet before it whirls down the drain. The sound of rain hitting a roof, falling against a car window, pelting an umbrella.

This is one of my great losses. While I can hear things, my discrimination is not strong enough to pick up more subtle sounds. And when I can, amplified by my hearing aids, it's not genuine sound, not with something as ephemeral as the sound of water. I'm lucky to hear all of the things that I do, but some things, like water, I so long to hear the real, natural sound of.

Waves washing over my feet, Olive enthusiastically lapping up water in that insatiable way that dogs do.

I wonder if I'd love these sounds as much if I hadn't lost them, but, because I have, I remember to appreciate the other ways that I experience things. Slipping into a hot bath, the steam rising around me as I sink in; walking out into the waves in Hawaii, the combined smell of flowers and suntan lotion mixed with salt. The icy water that I chug after my spin classes.

As much as I miss sounds, though, I have learned to love silence even more.

When I think back on all of the noise I grew up with and how comfortable I was with sound, I am amazed at how significantly my circumstances and feelings about sound have changed. If I had a choice, I'd definitely choose to be deaf rather than blind.

I used to be terribly afraid of the dark and of silence. I remember when my brothers and I would sit under the watchful eyes of our parents during high holiday services. Knowing that we were supposed to be completely silent made it that much more challenging to do so. A simple look from one of my brothers would send me into such hysterics that I'd slide down in my seat and drop my head forward so that my long hair would cover my face, while shoving as much of my fist in my mouth as I could to keep me from making a sound. My failed attempts to remain silent during these times were what I enjoyed most. As a child and a teenager, staying still and keeping quiet were not my strong suits.

Now, if I didn't have the ability to create silence for myself when I needed to, I'm pretty sure I'd lose my mind. Without the ability to turn off the noise, I think I would end up having a breakdown in the middle of the street amid the horns honking, the sirens blaring, and all of the other unnecessary sounds. I imagine myself climbing up onto the roof of a cab in traffic and yelling with as much force as I can, "SHUT THE FUCK UUUUUUUUPPPPP!!! EVERYONE! PLEASE! SHUT THE FUCK UP!!!" I'm a bit surprised that I haven't seen someone do this yet in the dozen years I've been living in this insanely noisy city.

My hearing aids often overamplify unwanted sounds and underamplify or distort the most important ones, creating a confusing mash of undifferentiated noise, or making it hard to focus. I am grateful that my hearing aids have enabled me to maintain my independence—without them, my life would be dramatically different and communicating every day would be a tremendous challenge. But it can really be a love/hate thing.

And while they deserve a great deal of recognition, oftentimes there is nothing better than taking them out.

How do I describe the sound of silence? Especially when the meaning of it has evolved for me so considerably over time. I focus so much of my time and energy on living presently and being in the moment, and I encourage the people I work with to do their best to live this way as well. When we spend too much time dwelling on the past or worrying about what may happen in the future, we lose sight of what it means to be alive. Yet, we are constantly bombarded by sound—the TV, music, phones ringing and texts beeping and people talking on them everywhere, horns honking, kids yelling, coffee grinding, etc. All of this makes it that much more difficult to be present without trying to escape or think about being in some other place and time.

Living with Usher syndrome has given me the blessing of silence. Each time I am able to take my hearing aids out and remove myself from the constant noise around me, I look up to whoever may be listening and think to myself, *Thank you, G-d!* I am not a particularly religious person but if I was, Silence would be the name of my religion.

Imagine yourself sitting in the middle of a Starbucks reading your book, working or really trying to focus on something, or maybe just trying to enjoy whatever coffee concoction you've chosen. Now imagine that a group of teenagers sits down at the table next to you, speaking in the loud, self-involved way that we swear we never spoke as teenagers, and you are lucky enough to get to hear them talk about the woes of their love lives or their grades in school. You likely look around to see if there are any free tables that you can move to, but of course, there aren't, so you silently will these teens to grab their caramel lattes and mocha Frappuccinos and head to their next hangout. Meanwhile, I have been sitting on the opposite side of the teens, removed my hearing aids and have been devoutly practicing my religion of Silence, with no idea or interest in what is going on around me. I am truly able to be with myself wherever I am, and without distraction, I can focus on whatever work I am doing or book I am reading, or simply luxuriate in my silence.

Silence seems to scare a lot of people: We live in a world that never seems to slow down or shut up, with a mind-boggling amount of entertainment and information right at our fingertips, and, if you stop to notice it, we are rarely in total quiet. Many of us have devices that create sound to drown out unwanted noise— noise to block noise. Perhaps silence should scare me, but it doesn't. Or maybe I've just accepted it and can truly appreciate its value.

I've also noticed that when I take out my ears, it's a time when my other senses really come to life. When I turn the water on to wash my face or to take a shower, I have nothing but my sense of touch and the use of my most central vision to experience the sensation of water—what it feels like against my skin, the temperature of it, and nothing else.

I often hear people say that they want to become more in touch with themselves—to have a stronger mind–body connection. My silence has allowed me to become more attuned to my thoughts, more connected to how I am feeling physically. We all need silence, but first, we need to become comfortable with not having noise and sound, which I think we have become incredibly uncomfortable living without. What does it mean when there is nothing to listen to, when there is nothing to distract yourself with? When there is nothing but you and silence?

People often pay a lot of money for the privilege of quiet. Some go away on weeks-long meditation retreats that are conducted in complete silence. Lucky me, all I have to do is take out my hearing aids.

48

If there is one thing that you absolutely need with a disability like mine, it is resilience. I'm not talking strong will and zest for life, either, but pure physical resilience. When you are going blind and deaf, you are basically an accident waiting to happen. There are countless dishwashers, cabinets, drawers, coffee tables, doors, tree branches, steel poles, etc. that I have smashed into, completely unaware of their existence. My body has become a shrine of scars and bruises: I stopped counting my scars a long time ago, and I can no longer look at a bruise and tell you how I got it. Caroline teases me about being a superhero because of how hard I slam into things at full speed and then just keep going. Because that's what you do, you just keep going.

If you've ever been to New York, you know the horror of the sidewalk cellar doors, metal doors in the ground that open to reveal sharp, steep staircases down to damp, dark basements that all New Yorkers avoid like the plague. Children are warned not to walk on them, lest they somehow open them and fall through. It is a common enough fear that when Samantha fell down one in a memorable *Sex and the City* episode, there was a shudder felt city-wide.

On Alan's fortieth birthday, after I was done teaching my last spin class I went to get my hair blown out while Caroline took care of Olive, waiting at my apartment so that we could get ready and go together. Alan and I weren't dating anymore and hadn't been for years, but I was still, of course, going to try to look my very best. Even though I was much happier with us just being friends, I had never gotten completely used to the idea of his dating other women. He is more generous in this regard than I am and has always been more than enthusiastic about wanting me to find someone wonderful to share my life with, though neither of us has ever had a relationship with anyone as remotely serious as we did with each other, either before or since. In any case, I still wanted to look great for his party.

It was not to be. By the time I left the salon it had started to rain, and it got heavier as I made my way home. The wind was blowing like crazy and I started to use my umbrella as a cane, rendering the blow-dry useless. The glare of the streetlights reflected back up at me from the puddles of water and blinded me, and I was so intent on trying to focus on what was right in front of me that I didn't see the open cellar to my side until my leg fell into it, scraping down the metal as it went. I caught myself with my arms just before I fell in completely and dangled there for a moment before I was able to pull myself up. My arms have always been strong—"Michelle Obama arms," one of my friends calls them—and I was so grateful for them right then. God knows what would have happened if I'd tumbled all the way down.

I climbed out and stumbled the last several blocks home, wiping at the blood that I could feel pouring out of the long cut on my leg. When I finally limped into the apartment, Caroline, used to but still irritated with my lateness, called out, "Took you long enough," and then walked into the room and let out a yell. Not much ruffles Caroline, but one look in the mirror told me why. I looked like Carrie, not from *Sex and the City* but from the Stephen King novel; I had managed to smear the blood I had been wiping off of my leg all over my face and hair, and the rain had helped it to seep into my clothes.

"I fell down a cellar," I told her, and burst into tears. Caroline understood immediately what I was talking about and went right into her calming mode, sitting me down and inspecting my leg, Olive hopping desperately around us. Olive, sadly, is not the kind of dog who will race to my side if I am crying, licking away my tears and trying to comfort me. Instead she'll seem confused and irritated that she is not getting the undivided attention she is certain she deserves, and will do her best to try and get it by dropping a toy in my lap and using her high-pitched yelp to get me to throw it. For once we ignored her, because a good look at my leg told Caroline that it was cut close to the bone, and that I should go straight to the emergency room, like a normal person. But I'm not.

It hurt like a bitch and was pouring more blood than we would have liked, but this was Alan's fortieth, and we both knew it was going to take a lot more than that for me to miss celebrating one of my very best friends. We were already running late, and any ER in New York City takes hours and hours. And honestly, what was one more scar? I wore them like battle wounds, and had grown so used to the sight of them that I barely noticed them anymore. So we got the blood off of me and triaged the cut as best we could. Caroline cleaned it as thoroughly as any doctor would have, and then bandaged it up tightly with many layers of gauze and medical tape. I have medical supplies for every emergency—burns, cuts, you name it, it happens to me on a regular basis.

Because Caroline is Caroline, she didn't push me to go to the hospital. I'm sure other people would have, and Alan would have had me in the emergency room in five minutes, but she knows that for me, missing things because of my disabilities is unbearable. So she just took care of it, and me, to the best of her ability, and I trusted her to, because Caroline is probably the most competent person I know.

I traded the short dress I was going to wear for a long one and tried my best to fix the thick, snarled mess that was now my hair. We went and I had a great time, despite the deep throbbing in my leg. I never went to the ER. Just one more scar to add to my collection.

49

I used to be the most sighted of the blind people, the best-hearing of the deaf. I could help other people find their lost things and interpret for a deaf person in sign language. Over the years, I have always dreaded my hearing and vision assessments. There is only one purpose for them: to chart my decline. I know what the sum-up is going to be: Your hearing is getting worse. Your vision is getting worse. You're not deaf and blind yet, but you're a little further along. Now I was in another doctor's office, for more tests. Tests I was prepared to fail. This time, though, failure wasn't necessarily a bad thing. This time was different, and I wasn't alone. Caroline and Alan were there, too. There was no way they would miss this.

. . . .

In January of 2013, I got a message from NYU Langone telling me that I might now qualify as a candidate for a cochlear implant, a surgically implanted electronic device that allows some people who are deaf or severely hard of hearing to "hear" again, though "experience sound" is probably more accurate, because, being digitized, it sounds vastly different from natural hearing. I was shocked. Twice in the previous five years Alan had persuaded me to go to New York Eye and Ear Infirmary of Mt. Sinai, to the doctor who he had read was the very best, to see if I qualified. I was told both times that I was not a candidate and that, although someday I would be, it was still something way down the road, a far-off idea for when I was much closer to total deafness. But after a couple of friends who also had Usher syndrome type III were implanted at NYU, I had gone to them to find out if I qualified.

It had always been something so distant that I couldn't ever really imagine it. When I was young the implants weren't nearly as powerful and advanced as they have become, and they were big, bulky, and hard to wear. It had all seemed so far away, the way that completely losing my vision and hearing had. Now, though, the powers that be were telling me that I might really be deaf, or deaf enough. Of course, though, they would have to do more tests to find out. There are *always* more tests.

If I could have all the days that I've spent having my eyes and ears tested back, it would be at least a year, probably more, and still, a part of me has never gotten over the feeling that I can somehow affect the tests' outcome, that if I just concentrated more, tried harder, gave it my all, I would be able to do better on them.

. . . .

My first reaction to the idea of the implant was not one that I had expected. Alan, my parents, and most everybody else were over-the-moon excited. Alan immediately began researching the makes and models of implants and made sure his schedule was free for my initial appointments. This was it, my implant! I would have a bionic ear and be able to hear again forever. My hearing would be cured! That had become the general reaction from others, before I even had my first intake appointment. But who could blame them? It sounded so perfect from an outsider's perspective; who wouldn't want the chance to hear again?

Caroline, though, immediately understood how I was feeling. She came right over when I told her, made sure she could be there on the day of my first evaluation, took one look at the apprehension on my face, and listened.

I was terrified. First of all, it would mean drilling a hole in my head. Hole. In. My. Head. Second, any natural hearing I had in that ear would likely be wiped out permanently. There was a lot I didn't know, but I knew that my mother's voice would never again sound like her voice to me. I also knew that, if I did turn out to be a candidate, it would mean that my disabilities had advanced to a new level. If I was being honest with myself, I recognized that my hearing had gotten worse over the past several years. It's hard for me to gauge the small changes, the way we don't notice ourselves aging when we look in the mirror from day to day. I never thought that it had gotten bad enough for me to qualify for a cochlear implant and that it might now be a better option than a hearing aid. While I knew people who had successfully had the surgery and seen their lives improve greatly from it, I also knew others who hated it because, even with time, the hearing sounded so foreign and indecipherable that they never wore it again. The ones who didn't use it were mostly people I knew who had been deaf or profoundly deaf since birth, and who found the noise so overwhelming and hard to adapt to that they decided to forget hearing altogether and rely completely on sign.

I knew that because I was able to hear and understand authentic sound, my chances were better, but it didn't lessen my fear.

The day of my first test was freezing cold and windy, and I could barely see as Alan and I made our way down to NYU Langone Medical Center. Caroline, who was now working as a social worker at Bellevue hospital, had raced over during her lunch break to meet us and was waiting for us in the lobby. We made our way upstairs to the waiting room, with Alan talking excitedly about all the cochlear research he'd been doing and the pros and cons of different brands, and Caroline scanning my expression to see how I was doing. When we got to the waiting room, she and I left our mountain of puffy coats and overstuffed backpacks on grown-up chairs next to Alan and sat down at one of the kids' tables, in chairs that were a suitable size for kindergarteners, mixing and matching Mr. Potato Head's ears, eyes, and feet. I had just gotten him all dressed up in his top hat and mustache when the audiologist came in and called out my name.

She introduced herself as Laurel and led us down the hall to a standard audiologist's office, sound booth and all.

"Are you ready to record your next album, Ms. Streisand?" Alan inquired, and I gave him my best singing-diva face.

Laurel gave us the basics on what the surgery involved, the different implants that I could choose from, the statistics on outcomes. She whipped out an ear diagram and pointed to the cochlea, then to the auditory nerve, said the word "electrodes" a few times, and put it away. Or at least that's what I caught.

"I'm ready to do the exam!" I announced, the science flying by me, even though I knew I should be trying harder to listen. I also knew that Alan and Caroline, my faithful ears, were busy writing everything down and asking the important questions. I never had to worry about that when they were there; Alan probably already knew as much as the audiologist. I'm convinced that his true calling was to be a doctor or a researcher.

When I went into the booth it was the usual drill. I raised my hand every time I heard a beep. At first I could hear everything, and my hand would fly up proudly. Then, I couldn't. I could tell by the timing that I was missing a lot. Another test I was going to bomb.

Then it was on to word discrimination, where a prerecorded man with a low-pitched voice says words that I'm supposed to repeat back. I hate this part; it never goes well. Caroline wrote down a few and told me later what the real words were, and it went something like this:

"*Popcorn.*" I heard something that sounded like "mopmop," so I shrugged my shoulders with a stupid grin on my face at Laurel, who was facing me outside of the booth, and told her that I didn't know.

"*Toothbrush.*"

"Toothbrush!"

"*Mailman.*"

"Handheld!"

"*Hot dog.*"

"Hot diggity dog!"

Then I was really unable to hear them and started guessing. Caroline wrote them down, because that's what she does, but also because she knew that they would make me laugh later, even though I was trying hard not to cry now.

"Um, 'ostrich' or 'tobacco.'

"'Loose,' 'goose,' 'moose'?

"'Fish,' 'dish,' 'wish'?

"That sounded like 'fog' or 'blanket.'

"'Spaghetti' or 'porcupine'?

"Hmm, that sounds like 'fuck,' but I don't think that's the word you're giving me. Sorry for the language."

When I came out I tried to smile for Alan and Caroline, but they weren't fooled. They knew I'd be crying when we left. It's harder with the prerecorded voice, which I hadn't been tested with in a long time—it's often the audiologist who does it, which is easier to understand—and I knew that I hadn't done well. My stomach curled up as I waited to hear the results.

The last time, with the audiologist reading, I had scored a 74 percent in my left ear and 44 in my right. Today, Laurel told me, my left ear had 40 percent discrimination and the right just 26 percent. This meant, she explained, that I was likely a candidate for an implant. Alan looked thrilled; clearly, doing badly was a good thing. Laurel handed us marketing materials from all three cochlear implant device companies, full of photographs of smiling children and families, along with a ten-page questionnaire for me to fill out. Of course, to add insult to injury, the questionnaire was in very small print. Awesome.

When we got home, Alan started reading me the questions, but after the first couple of pages I was so tired and overwhelmed by the day that I could barely concentrate. I knew that they could answer most of them for me anyway, so I curled up on the couch with Olive against my belly and let them do it. This is what it means to have devoted friends. They will fill out a ten-page questionnaire in teeny tiny print for you, and they will know the answers to questions like:

Does your tinnitus cause problems in your family?

On a scale from 1 to 100 does your tinnitus do this or that?

I must have fallen asleep for a little while, because I awoke to them laughing, so bored that they had started making up their own questions.

Do you find your tinnitus hogs the covers at night?

Does your tinnitus constantly leave the toilet seat up?

Does your tinnitus drink milk straight from the carton?

. . . .

A week later I had a CAT scan, and then I got the call a few weeks after that: I now qualified for a cochlear implant.

50

Dr. J. Thomas Roland, the chairman of otolaryngology at NYU Langone, who would be performing the cochlear implant surgery, is one of those people who exudes so much competence that you could actually trust him to drill a hole in your head. As I sat in his office while he explained the process to me, his calm, deep voice and big, capable hands would have been reassuring if I hadn't been so terrified. Alan and Peter were with me and listened, enthralled, nodding at the right moments, while I sat completely still and gripped the armrests of my chair. One of the few times I'm not fidgety is when I'm scared.

Dr. Roland told us that he would be making an opening behind my ear, so he could drill a small hole on the surface of my skull, just under my scalp, where the implant would be nestled. The implant, which is about the size of a silver dollar, is then connected by a thin wire to electrodes that would be carefully inserted deep inside my ear, snaked around the tiny, snail-shaped cochlea, inside of which most of my hair cells are now dead. Usher syndrome has killed nearly all of them. In a normal ear, those thousands of hair cells convert sound into electrical impulses that travel via the auditory nerve to the brain.

Once he closed me up, I would get all the external gadgets that I needed in order to communicate with the implant. There was a headpiece, a small round cap that would magnetically adhere to my head at the site of the implant, which would then be connected to a sound processor that would take the noise of the outside world and send it into my head. My right ear would be essentially decorative at that point, as the electrodes deep inside my inner ear would now and forever do the job of my dearly departed hair cells.

Even though my right ear was growing increasingly useless, I took some comfort in knowing that if a bomb went off, I could still probably hear it. The cochlea is extremely delicate, and even though Dr. Roland was the best of the best, once he snaked that electrode array into it, whatever few hair cells I had left would probably be too traumatized to survive. Thus, my right ear would become completely bionic. He explained that preserving inner ear function is more and more possible these days, and that the surgery and recovery are generally very easy, and I should be able to go home within a day. Apparently my auditory nerve was fine, and I was an ideal patient, and, because I'd had decades of hearing, the process of relearning how to hear electronically should be fast, which meant the sounds should start to make sense again fairly quickly, and I would be able to hear things again that I hadn't heard in decades. He said with confidence that this should happen within a few days to a few weeks, and that it would just keep getting better and better over time.

He told us that though right now I could understand less than a quarter of the words spoken to me, after the surgery that number should eventually go up to 85 or 90 percent, maybe even more. Also, he said that by three months after the implant is turned on, 85 to 90 percent of people feel that their tinnitus is suppressed. *Just this once,* I thought, *let me please, please, be in the majority.*

This is what he told us, and Alan and Peter, and everyone we told afterward, were jubilant.

But this is what I heard: We are going to drill a big hole in your head. I didn't want a big hole drilled in my head. I remembered all of the surgeries after my accident and was sick at the thought of having to go through all the pain and grogginess and recovery. Intellectually, I knew that this would be a much smaller surgery with far less recovery time, but emotionally that information wasn't helping. Then they were going to put a device in my head large enough that I would be able to feel it. Feel it on the outside of my head, under the skin. On the outside, the piece that connected the implant to the little box that transmitted the hearing would attach to my head *magnetically.* Like on a fridge. I wondered briefly if a little fridge magnet would be able to stick to my head, too. I knew that Caroline and I would end up trying it.

If everyone had been excited before, things had now reached a fever pitch. Word spread quickly, and every family member and friend reached out, so excited for me. There are tons of YouTube videos of people having their cochlear implants turned on for the first time. Toddlers who've never heard before looking up in wonder as they hear their parents' voices. Or a mother hearing her children, her eyes widening with joy. You can't help but cry; it's amazing.

Except, it's not that easy. In fact, it's not like that at all. Yes, they are hearing sound, and, especially if you've never heard anything before, that is extraordinary, but it in *no way* resembles any kind of thing that we would associate with a "voice." For many people, especially those who've had hearing previously, after a period of adjustment, a voice will start to sound like a voice, a dog's bark a bark, a song a song, though even when it does, there is an artificial quality that never goes away. It might seem like a small price to pay, but it doesn't feel like it when you're on the receiving end.

The two other women I know with Usher III, Wendy and Cindy, who had both been implanted, urged me to do it, saying it was the best thing they'd ever done and that they both wished that they'd done it years ago. Wendy told me that after she was implanted, she went to see the movie *Lincoln* and heard almost every word, and I knew that was about the wordiest movie ever. That seemed so far beyond my reach that I found it impossible to imagine that *that* could be me. Also, my disabilities had always seemed to be years behind theirs, much less advanced. Maybe I wasn't ready, maybe I should wait, I kept thinking to myself, trying to give logic to my fears.

Implants are also a very controversial thing in the deaf community. Part of the reason is that the deaf already have their own language and a very rich and lively culture, and don't consider deafness to be a disability. Another is that it doesn't work for every kind of deafness. Still another is that for many people who have never had hearing, it is unbearable noise, and, after the difficult surgery and mapping process, they are never able to discriminate sounds to recognize what they're hearing except loud noise.

Cochlear implants are wildly expensive, too. I knew I was so lucky to be able to have surgery to improve my quality of life, surgery that my insurance would mostly be covering, and that my family and I had the means to pay for the rest of it, which so many people do not. I knew I needed to stop freaking out and just be grateful and hope for the best.

Of all of my friends and family, only Daniel was a voice of dissent. He urged me to consider acupuncture, to do meditation and yoga, assured me that he and I and many others could cure ourselves of our ailments. I wanted to ask him how that was going for him, but instead I just became vague and noncommittal and decided I wouldn't talk about it with him again. I was scared enough as it was, and I could understand Danny's perspective, when he had tried so many Western medicines and procedures, to no avail. I knew that he just wanted to try to protect me.

I also knew that Daniel was stuck and had been unable to make any kind of move to help himself change that. I see so many people who are stuck: in their jobs, their grief, their relationships, their anger. People who, for whatever reason, can't move on. In my practice, I do my best to help them become unstuck and move forward. To help them recognize whatever it is that's holding them back from the life that they want, and to help them get past what's holding them back.

Unfortunately there is no way to simply get "past it," "over it," or "around it"; the only way is to go "through it." Or for those who like catchphrases, you have to "feel it to heal it." In my life, I've never done anything that I'm proud of without having to work tirelessly at it. As far as I can tell, there are no shortcuts to this process, just work. Just doing it every day. I push my patients to break through these barriers; I push my spin classes to work harder, to get past what they believe their limits are and find out what they are truly capable of.

People tend to get so stuck in the unhappiness of their lives because it's familiar, and they find comfort in the discomfort because it's predictable and what they know. Breaking that cycle requires you to face your fears, to explore the unknown, and to *let yourself be afraid and vulnerable.*

So, despite my fears and apprehensions, I decided to schedule my surgery for the earliest date that I could: May. Right after I did I wanted to put it off for longer but I didn't, because I knew that there was never going to be a "right" time to do it, and I wasn't just going to wake up one morning and feel ready for it. My family was already making their plans to come, rescheduling their lives so they could be there for me, and working it out so that my mom's and dad's time with me didn't overlap. All that was left was to get my vaccinations, get my work in order for the time off, and wait.

Alan was deep into implant research, laying out the pros and cons for me. My thoughts and anxieties piled on top of one another. The what-ifs came rapid-fire, and I couldn't, at first, remember a single reason why this was a good idea.

As the date drew closer, I felt more and more scared. And that's when I realized: *I* was stuck. I had so many fears, and, even more, so much sadness that this day had come and that my Usher was so far advanced. I really was becoming the girl who was blind and deaf. The implant would almost surely make my life better. It would undoubtedly eventually make it easier. But the devil I knew was still drowning out the brave voice, the one that knew I should do it. I had only been able to focus on the negative, because I was so scared.

I knew what I needed to do, which was to follow the advice that I give to my patients: acknowledge the loss, and allow myself to be in the present and feel the sadness and the fear, so that I can move into the future.

When I was younger I never understood that I would lose this much and never really believed that my hearing would get this bad. Now it had happened, but I was afraid to let go of what I did have: genuine sounds. Amplified where I didn't want them sometimes, and too quiet for the things I did want to hear at others, but my mother's voice was her voice, and Caroline's laugh was her laugh, and Olive's annoyingly loud bark was her bark, and I knew that it wouldn't ever be the same again with the implant. If I had a child, I would never hear her genuine cry or the authentic sound of her voice. They'd tinker until the implant approximated sounds as best as it could, but it wouldn't ever be real again. That is what plagued me most.

Then, I admit, came the more shallow thoughts: I didn't want them to shave a part of my head. Everyone would see the implant if I was wearing a ponytail, which I pretty much always do. I'd also have a little device that I'd have to put somewhere. I'd look like I was in the Secret Service; I couldn't decide if that was better or worse than looking like I had a cochlear implant. I was a single woman in New York, and an implant (coupled with a cane) is decidedly not sexy or pretty, though Alan kept saying that it didn't matter, that I was gorgeous and nobody would care and if they did, fuck them. If only all men thought that way.

Then, finally, the other voice inside of me, which had been patiently waiting its turn, waiting until I was ready to hear what it had to say, told me, "Yes, but you'll be able to hear." I'd be able to hear. I wouldn't check out in the middle of dinner. I'd be quick and witty again, not just in texts or emails but right there, at the table, making people laugh and laughing the first time someone told a joke. I'd be able to go to the movies, and they'd be more than just an expensive nap.

Helping other people, quite literally, helps me. It makes me better able to accept help. It empowers me, gives structure to my world. It lets me know that I am useful and able, and it feels so good. It has always felt good, but as I grow to need more help, I need that feeling more. The implant, the idea of which kept me up at night fretting, would help me to do that. I would be able to keep my practice, even when I was completely blind. Even if my clients' voices sounded like Alvin, Simon, and Theodore's, or like aliens', I'd have the word discrimination to hear them. Even if I hated the sound, I would hear the words and remain truly able to listen.

I repeated these things to myself when I had trouble sleeping. Breathe in peace, breathe out fear. *I'll always be able to listen to and really hear my patients; I won't have to stop my practice someday.* Breathe in peace, breathe out fear. *I won't have to say "what" (I hope) fifty times a day anymore.* Breathe in peace, breathe out fear. *I have recovered from so many things—my accident, my eating disorder—and I have dealt with my disabilities as they have gotten worse, and this is a good thing. A scary thing, but a good thing.* Breathe in peace, breathe out fear.

I could have waited on the cochlear implant, until one was "completely implantable"—meaning it wouldn't show. I considered it, but it could have been two years or more until that was available, and I qualified now. I knew that it would be a disservice to me, to my patients, and to the people who loved me to wait. It is human nature to believe there is always going to be something better in the future, but I couldn't live for then, I had to live for now. I had to make choices now, and my choice was yes, I would get the implant now.

. . . .

A few days before the surgery I had an MRI on my right knee, which had been hurting for the past several months. Once I was implanted I would never be able to have one again, because there would be metal in my body permanently. The news from the doctor wasn't surprising: I had been favoring my right knee ever since the accident, and there was nothing to be done about the joint pain. He suggested using it less, which clearly wasn't an option, and referred me to a physical therapist. I promised to see him just as soon as I found the time, wondering when on earth that might happen.

Two days before my surgery, after I had seen my last patient, I closed my office door behind me before quickly reopening it to take one last look—I wanted to be sure I had everything and that I'd left the space tidy and inviting to come back to. I wasn't sure when that would be—just a couple of weeks, I hoped, though it would most likely be at least a month. I had originally thought I could go back to work within a week, but I was quickly disabused of this notion.

Leading up to my surgery, what I had mostly said to people about it was that I was "getting a hole in my head." I knew it sounded silly, but it was the only way I knew how to tell others without having to reveal my sadness and fear about the whole process. Caroline and I would joke about "pimping my implant" and she promised to get a BeDazzler and make it all snazzy.

As I walked home, the streets around me were mostly deserted with the exception of a handful of people walking their dogs and a couple of men in suits carrying briefcases with a look of exhaustion on their faces and in their shoulders. I was happy to have the sidewalk mostly to myself. When I got home, Olive greeted me with her usual overwhelming enthusiasm, as though she hadn't seen me in weeks. Her tail wagged vigorously as she rested her front paws on my knees and licked my face. It was one of the only times when even my sweet little Monkey couldn't pull me out of my funk, though her warm body against mine couldn't help but make me feel a little better.

The sense of loneliness and sadness overwhelmed me, though, and I knew what I needed to do: mourn what I was losing. Say good-bye to my ear. When I'm alone, I often feel most comforted by taking a bath. It's a typical New York tub: not long enough for me to straighten my legs, and not as deep as I'd like, but still, sliding my body into the warm water calmed my body and my mind, and as I lay there, with my head back and my eyes closed, and felt the warmth of the water softly embrace my whole body, I finally relaxed and let the tears come. They started slowly, but before long I was sobbing, letting it all out: the fear, the sorrow, and the hope, too, putting it all out there. I touched my ear and apologized to it. I know that might sound silly or strange, but I was sorry. It had done the best it could, and it would never be able to do its job again. I was apologizing to myself, and I was crying out of exhaustion. I was so tired of trying to keep up with everyone and live my life like everybody else, as though I was fully hearing and sighted. I knew, too, that I had many months of worse exhaustion ahead of me, and I hoped—prayed—that things would get easier. That's why I was doing this, to make my quality of life better.

51

On the morning of the surgery, Caroline, my mom, Alan, and I arrived at the hospital at six thirty. I hadn't slept much, was terrified, and, awesome, I had a UTI. I changed into my hospital gown while Caroline, ever vigilant, put things away, keeping everything off the floor and as MRSA-free as possible. She had brought my pillow for me, and it was double pillowcased and tied tightly inside a garbage bag. I flashed Alan my hospital-provided granny panties from the exposed back of my gown. He rolled his eyes, Caroline cracked up, and my mother scolded me.

Dr. Roland came in and I tried to stay calm. *Breathe in peace, breathe out fear.* I was still worried about the implant that I'd chosen, wondering if I should have gone with a different one, second-guessing myself about a decision I'd made weeks before.

My mom and Alan kept the doctor busy, peppering him with questions. Alan asked about the medication and whether it would make me constipated. It was like having two Jewish mothers in there with me. After that Caroline signed only the important questions to me, because she could tell that at that point I was happy to let them take over. She climbed into the reclining chair with me, and I put my head on her as Alan rubbed my feet. I needed to be touched right then, to feel anchored. Then I got up and did push-ups and triceps dips and wall sits, trying to calm myself down. Caroline tried in her own goofy way to help, too, putting on my operating cap and blowing up the plastic gloves into five-finger balloons.

Soon the anesthesiologist came in and talked to me, and I made it clear that the thing I was most concerned about was the pain medication. I hadn't forgotten the excruciating pain of my accident, and I just wanted there to be lots and lots of drugs waiting for me when I was done.

When it came time for me to go, my mom and Caroline and Alan all took turns reassuring me, and then the nurse wheeled me off to the elevator, not letting me walk. *Nobody gets to walk,* she told me. While I waited to be wheeled into the OR, Dr. Roland chatted with me, probably trying to calm my nerves, telling me about his son graduating from college and what he and his family would be doing for Memorial Day weekend. When they finally wheeled me in and I lay down on the cold operating table, I wished that I had one of Lisa's music mixes, but, of course, I thought with half a smile, I couldn't hear it anyway. I asked them to please not count back from ten when it was time for the anesthesia, and I lay back and closed my eyes, *Breathe in peace, breathe out fear,* and the next thing I remembered was waking up, sick and groggy, and asking the nurse if I could have someone come up to help me communicate, since I no longer had any hearing in my right ear and I wasn't wearing my left hearing aid because my whole head was wrapped in a bandage, turban style. I didn't have my glasses, and my eyes were blurry from the drugs. She was impatient with me, telling me to sit quietly and that she would get an interpreter, but I knew that I needed my mother or Caroline, that I was not in any kind of shape to talk, let alone sign, with a stranger. I felt so helpless and disabled in that moment, and I needed someone who really knew how to communicate with *me*.

Caroline told me later that she was frantic to get to me after my surgery—she knew that I would need her—and that she finally just ignored the nurse and came anyway, brushing past people and into the recovery room. I grabbed her hand, relief coursing through me. In this moment, I saw a flash of what my life could have been like, completely blind and deaf and walled off from the world, having absolutely no real way to communicate. It was so terrifying that it briefly cut through my wooziness, and in a momentary flash I understood what a gift this implant was, and what it was saving me from.

We were able to go home later that day, but for the next two weeks I felt dizzy and fragile, and there was much more pain than I had expected. My mother stayed with me for the first week, sleeping on the couch and taking care of me. My mom is one of the only people whom I can let take care of me completely. She cooked, cleaned, and wrote down the food menu for the day on a large, white dry-erase board. For one of the first times in my life, though, I felt unable to eat. Nothing seemed to work for the nausea and vertigo, until a friend brought me some pot cookies, and it was clear to me five minutes after the first bite that medical marijuana should be legalized right away.

Two days later, Caroline made a whole contraption to wash my hair. She set up pillows in the bathroom, put a huge garbage bag over all of them, and got in the bathtub to wash my hair. It reminded me of my accident, but this time I wasn't looking forward to it. I didn't want to unwind my turban, and when I did I wouldn't look at the surgery site, though my Mom and Caroline told me enthusiastically that it looked great! Much better than expected! They finally took a picture of it on the phone to show me, and I saw that they were right. The sutures where the scar would be were well hidden behind my ear, and though the other people I knew who had been implanted had to have a large spot on their head shaved, mine was very small.

. . . .

Over the next couple of weeks I kept my hearing aid out of my other ear as much as possible, because hearing from only one side is mostly nauseating and confusing, like having one ear completely clogged after an airplane flight, a feeling that I prayed would pass, because once the implant was turned on I was supposed to use it solo much of the time, to help me adjust. The sounds I heard coming through it would be so distinctly different from the way they sounded through my hearing aid that the doctor and audiologist had told me that I should get used to the implant before integrating both. I walked around like a drunk teenager, unable to keep my balance without holding on to someone.

I couldn't imagine how different everything would sound once my implant was turned on, but I tried to remind myself that everyone hated it in the beginning and that I had to be patient.

I'm so fortunate, I told myself. Modern medicine was on my side; it was rooting for me, giving me the blessing of hearing, and maybe, maybe, someday, the blessing of sight, though I couldn't fathom being fully hearing and sighted any more than I could imagine being completely blind or deaf.

52

Three weeks after the surgery, I went in to have my implant turned on. That morning, Alan and Polly crowded into the small audiologist's office with me. They were so clearly excited and hopeful, and I sat down, squeezing my hands tightly together to try to relieve my anxiety a little. I was still so afraid of what my new ear was going to sound like and of hearing completely differently for the rest of my life. Laurel gave me the magnetic headpiece to place on the side of my head, and I held it there until she told me to let go. It stayed put. At first I was afraid to turn my head or make any sudden movements, but I soon realized that it was held fast by the magnet inside my head. I wondered aloud if other things were going to stick to it, and she joked that I might feel pulled to the fridge when I was near it. *I'm already attracted enough to the fridge,* I thought, but I knew my voice would shake too much to pull off a joke right then.

Before Laurel turned on the implant she assured me that whatever I heard would be normal and that my brain would adjust in time. The room was silent as she turned it on, and the first sounds started to come through. I couldn't tell yet what I was hearing. I felt a pulsing like I would during a hearing test; it was as though I could both hear and feel the reverberations from the side of my head. Laurel and I were signing to one another as she sent me tones, which all sounded high and eerie. Then she spoke: "We're on. Can you hear me?"

It was shocking. I felt as though I had just unknowingly walked into a room full of people who'd yelled, "Surprise!" and my brain was trying to catch up with what was happening. So naturally, the first words that came from my mouth were: "That is fucked up." I apologized to Laurel as I covered my mouth with my hand, and then said it again, my own voice sounding unbelievably strange. "Is that me?" I asked, though of course it was, but my brain just wasn't understanding. Everything sounded very high-pitched and monotone, and initially it seemed as though their voices were coming to me from inside my head. Alan started to talk and his voice sounded so high that I whipped around in my chair. "Holy shit! Is that you?" He laughed and it sounded squeaky and evil. Like a high-pitched, cackling devil. The tone of his voice sounded *exactly* the same as the tone of Laurel's voice. I was stupefied. *Have I given up my little bit of real sound for something completely robotic and digitized and . . . creepy? Don't cry, breathe in peace, breathe out fear.* I had a feeling I was saying "fuck" more than people generally do, so I tried to mostly sign it.

My tinnitus was still there but it was drowned out a bit by the fact that my new hearing seemed to be coming from the same place my tinnitus does. Half of me wanted to rip the implant out of my head, but the other was hugely curious to find out what this crazy thing could do.

Laurel took me through several words. "Baseball." "Ice cream." "Popcorn." I somehow managed to get most of them right, not because I was able to hear the words as much as I was able to discriminate how many syllables were being spoken. I was blown away that I could distinguish anything at all on the first day. I heard her say, "I like ice cream," so I repeated it back to her, and when she nodded her head at me to let me know I'd gotten it right, I couldn't help but feel like this was some kind of a game or sport that I could be really good at if I practiced. I thought to myself, *I am going to work as hard as I can to rock this thing.*

After the testing she took the headpiece off and began to take it apart to show me how to care for it. There were an unbelievable number of things to remember—buttons, lights, batteries, one thing clicking into something else, magnets, a swim cover—all for such a small device. Well, small until it was attached to me; then it felt gigantic. She was telling me a million different things and I was catching very little of it, because I was still so over-whelmed and only had my hearing aid in my left ear, but I knew that Polly was taking careful notes and Alan was watching every-thing with his usual laser-beam attention. He loves gadgets, and this is one to end all gadgets. He knows so much more than I do about all of this stuff that *he* should be the deaf one.

Caroline finally showed up, racing from work, and I just wanted to hand it all to her to figure out and take a nap. I was still reeling from the sounds, and I didn't want to put the headpiece back on when Laurel handed it back to me. She told me that I should wear it all day and take out my hearing aid for at least an hour or two to practice listening with it on its own.

Laurel also told me that I should try my best not to lipread. She said that I was better at it than anyone she'd ever met, which seemed unlikely to me, because I have less vision than most, but I loved hearing it, because in my world it's a coveted skill. I wanted to lipread, though, I love it, but she explained that it would hinder me from learning to hear with just my implant. Lipreading has been somewhat of a lifeline for me, and it is a huge part of how I hear, so although I'd have loved to be able to hear without it, I still couldn't imagine that it was possible.

As we were leaving, Laurel called out, "Oh, I almost forgot, no signing! Try to rely on the implant completely for now." *What?* As soon as we thanked her and got into the elevator, Caroline and I started signing. To not sign or lipread at all right then seemed impossible. I needed to explain to Caroline how I was feeling, and signing was the best way for me to do that. "No signing!" Alan chided, and Caroline shot him a glare. This is typical Alan and Caroline. They both want to support me but go about it in wildly different ways.

When Alan and I got back to my apartment, I took off my hearing aid and just had the implant on, and I could understand some of what he was saying, which I didn't even notice until he pointed it out. It didn't sound remotely like him, and every time he laughed he sounded like a demon, and I had no idea how it was making sense, because it didn't even seem as though I was using the same part of my brain that I usually did to hear. It was as though it was going through another channel altogether, but nevertheless, I seemed to . . . hear him? That didn't feel like what it was. To be able to discriminate some of the words? To understand him.

Laurel had said that people should read to me as much as possible, but to start with simple things. I remembered that Cindy told me that she watched a lot of soap operas to relearn sound, because the simple, dramatic dialogue was easy to understand and follow. That sounded unbearable to me, so instead, over the next week, Polly read me *People* and *Real Simple* and other magazines. I heard about Paris Jackson's suicide attempt and how

Kate and Will were preparing for their baby. I got tips about re-organizing the kitchen, or maybe it was prioritizing; I wasn't hearing that one as clearly.

That first night, Caroline slept over, and before we went to bed she sat next to me, and, for the first time *ever*, she was on my right side. She read me *The Runaway Bunny*, and I was like a child, relearning from the most basic of words. She read slowly, enunciating each word carefully, and when she finished we snuggled with Olive, who planted herself firmly between us. *Good night, my little bunny*, I told Olive. I had made it through the first day. *Breathe in peace, breathe out fear.*

53

Six months after my surgery, what I could hear with my co-chlear implant was remarkably different from what I heard during my first few months of bionic hearing. The sounds were no longer all high-pitched and monotone; I had much more discrimination, though everything still sounded robotic.

Hearing has been hard work for me for such a long time now—I don't know that I've been able to hear anything easily since childhood—and I have had to keenly focus whenever I want to hear what's being spoken or what's happening around me. It can be so exhausting that I often end up tuning things out when it becomes too big a struggle. I hate to accept defeat and do that, but sometimes it's just too hard.

Learning how to hear with a cochlear implant, at first, complicated the hearing process even more, because the sound is digitized. That means that not only did I have to intently listen, I also had to try to discriminate and make sense of the new type of sound I was hearing. During the first six months of activation, people are encouraged to either go to bed two hours earlier each night or to take a nap during the day because it can be so exhausting. Most of the time I wished I had time for both.

Although I still struggle quite a bit to hear—hearing with one acoustic ear and one bionic ear has been the hardest part of this process, because the sound my brain is processing simultaneously with both ears is completely different—my discrimination with my implanted ear has improved tremendously. At almost three months after my activation, I had my first official post-implant hearing test. Before I had been implanted, my right ear had only 26 percent discrimination with the use of a hearing aid, and it had jumped to 76 percent since the surgery. Although I might not always feel like I hear 76 percent of what is being said to me, the numbers speak for themselves.

My left ear had been my stronger ear since I was a little girl unknowingly cocking it toward voices or the television. I had never used my right ear on the telephone; it was simply a lost cause. Now I use my right ear exclusively for it. Although the sound is still a bit distorted and will never sound like natural hearing to me, it is much more crisp and clear than the hearing I get with the help of a hearing aid. When people ask, I often tell them that the difference between using a hearing aid and using a cochlear implant is like the difference between hearing sound recorded on a poorly copied cassette tape versus hearing the same sound played on a CD.

It didn't happen overnight, though. It has come with countless hours of listening therapy, patient family and friends, and an eager brain. The most crucial component to this whole process has been my determination.

I thought I would be worried about how it looked, but I do not even have the time to think about it. Plus, my cane, which I use more and more now, is so much more obvious that I'm sure no one is paying attention to my ear.

54

I have found so many times in my life that there is no way to accept pain and sadness other than facing it head-on and allowing myself to feel it. I don't think most people can really move on unless they do that. Feelings are easy to bury, but they often come back even more strongly, or manifest themselves in far more destructive ways. We're so afraid to be vulnerable, to let ourselves feel deeply. We equate crying with weakness or childishness, but I think it's the opposite. Before children unlearn how to cry, they can express their emotions and then move on. If they fall down and skin a knee, or a friend hurts their feelings, they may cry, and then when they're done, it's over. I have so many patients who don't cry outside of my office, but who, when they finally let themselves break down, feel better afterward, relieved and more at peace.

That's how it was with the cane. I let myself hate it and be sad and cry. Then there were nights that started to come when I didn't cry (and some where I still did), but I would sometimes feel more confident, not less, with the cane's help. One of those nights, as

I made my way along the sidewalk, I noticed a woman walking close to me. I got to the street corner and waited for the crosswalk signal, and as soon as it changed she announced loudly, while looking straight ahead, "You can go now!"

Despite not being able to see the sidewalk, I could still see what was directly in front of me with ease. I wanted to tell her this, to say, "Thank you, but I don't need your help." But I didn't. I just made my way across the street, saying nothing.

Then she did it at the next light. And the next. I itched to say something, to show her that I wasn't really blind and that I was not in need of anyone's help. But I didn't. Instead I made myself do something that was one of the hardest things of all for me. I allowed myself to be blind and accept her help. I waited for her voice at each corner, and then, after several blocks of silence, I simply turned to her and said, "Thank you."

Those blocks of silence started out by making me feel incredibly uncomfortable. Part of me felt like I was lying by not letting on that I could see, at least a little bit, where I was going. Another part of me was desperate not to accept her help. I could see very little peripherally, but I knew there were other people who could see and hear us, and I was embarrassed. Then, as the blocks went on, I started to think, *So what?* I was only going to make life harder on myself by not accepting help. At some point, I was going to need this. Not just my friends and family, but the kindness of strangers. Already it was better for me to have a second set of eyes; if a car came flying through a light or around a corner I might not see it, but she would. I'm sure that she felt better knowing that she was helping me, and I needed to let myself feel better about it, too.

This, I realized when I got home, was as important a part of my training as the cane itself. Fact: Disabilities require help. Fact:

I hate help. The disabilities weren't going to change, so I was going to have to.

. . . .

Today, I love my cane. I still don't like taking it on dates, and I usually don't need it during the day, but it has now become indispensable to me at night. I feel more confident when I have it with me, and safer. I am not uncomfortable being alone, but walking down a dark street can be scary. I wonder now: When I have my cane, does it make me more or less vulnerable? Will a mugger or a rapist feel sorry for me and not want to rob or hurt a blind woman? Or does it just make me an easier target?

I always use it now when I'm traveling, if I'm at Penn Station or the airport. It makes things easier, and it generally alerts people to get out of my way. I used to be really self-conscious, but now I realize that I can't really see who's watching me anyway, and people are generally pretty helpful. So, I just have to go with it. I've also realized that people are never looking at you as much as you think they are. People are generally preoccupied with their own lives.

Perhaps my favorite thing about using my cane now is the type of responses and comments I get. While traveling, I have been asked several times by airport and train station agents whether I need assistance to my gate. When I tell them that I do, immediately their next question is, "Do you need a wheelchair?" Somehow people seem to have a difficult time keeping their disabilities straight. Luckily, my visual impairment does not impede my ability to walk. At these times, I have been tempted to say, "Uh, no, I'm likely in better shape than you are," but I don't. I simply say, "Nope, my legs work just fine."

55

When I met Peter and his wife Alison's infant daughter, my niece, Ava, I fell in love immediately. She was mine, my little darling, a gorgeous adventure for the senses. The gentle tenderness of her soft skin. Her sweet milky breath, warm on my face. I cupped her fragile, beautiful little head in my palm and touched the tip of her tiny nose and her rosebud lips. I felt the warmth of her forehead as I placed kiss after kiss upon it, and the little pitter-patter of her heart when I pressed her against me. She was, without a doubt, the most wonderful baby on earth. My mother and grandmother hovered around us, beaming, four generations crowded together, and I knew that they were both longing for this for me, wanting to huddle around my baby, to see me have everything that other women have.

· · · ·

My mom and I were on the phone recently as I was walking home from my office, exhausted after a long day with patients. My ears were ringing and worn out, and I had forgotten my cane, so my eyes strained to focus on the little bit of sidewalk I could see; I was glad it was a short walk that I was familiar with. We were catching up on all of our unimportantly important goings-on until the conversation finally took the turn it always does once I start to exhibit signs of wanting to hang up, one that I'm sure is familiar to many other single women in their thirties. It was time to entertain my mom's favorite subject: my love life.

"So, any men in your life these days?" she asked, just a bit too casually.

The dreaded yet entirely expected question. Oh yes, Mom, did I forget to mention that I just met the man of my dreams? It was not that there were no men in my life "these days," it was that there was nobody worth reporting home about, and I learned long ago that indulging my mom with the nuances of being single and dating in New York is like reading a fairy tale to a child who is hanging on my every word. So I told her about a date I had coming up with a guy I knew next to nothing about, except that he was attractive and had approached me at the gym while I was on the stair climber. As she pressed on for more details, I realized that she was already starting to play house with the idea of this new stranger whom I had idiotically introduced into our conversation. There was a strong likelihood that either he or I might cancel (in truth, probably me), but for the sake of my mom's hopes for my romantic happiness, and fervent desire that I will one day produce grandchildren, I feigned greater excitement over the whole thing.

"Whatever happened to Jon?" she asked. "You seemed to really like him." I rolled my eyes at nobody but myself, for not realizing that of course my mom wouldn't be satisfied with the fact that I was just going out on a date. She wanted me to be "proactive" about my love life and my future. My mother tells me constantly how proud she is of me, and I know that she just wants me to be happy and to have a full life. She wants my future to be secure—and, of course, her own future as the grandmother of my children—and she clearly doesn't see my disabilities as an impediment to any of this.

"You have a double master's from Columbia," she'll tell me, "that's an amazing accomplishment for anyone. Who wouldn't want to be with you? Your disabilities don't matter, you're so beautiful and smart and funny. Anyone who doesn't want to be with you is crazy."

When I arrived at my door, the conversation had wound down, as it generally does if I answer in the noncommittal affirmative on this subject for a while ("Mmmhmm. Uh-huh. Mmm . . ."). All I wanted to do was open the door to my sweet Olive and take my ears out, spending the couple of hours before bed in blissful silence, with all the puppy love I could handle.

"Well, I love you, Mama," I told her.

"I love you, too, sweet girl."

"Okay, talk to you soon."

"Yep, sounds good. Hey, Becky, you're thirty-four now, just to be safe you might want to look into freezing your eggs."

Really? How did my mom know that at ten P.M. on a Tuesday night, there was nothing I wanted to discuss more than freezing my eggs "just to be safe"? Are you fucking kidding me?

. . . .

As a child I never gave much thought to motherhood. I don't remember thinking about how many kids I'd have or giving much thought to whether I'd have them at all. I know that in New York egg freezing has become commonplace for women in their thir-ties, but until that moment I hadn't even considered the possibil-ity, let alone thought about the fact that I might get to a place where I was so desperate to have children that I would consider it.

The idea of my being a mom probably freaks some people out. It occasionally freaks me out. Or maybe it makes some people sad, because they couldn't fathom the idea that that's something I could do. I know that I would be an awesome mom, though. I have a tremendous amount of love and energy and compassion to share, and I love to teach and laugh. I adore kids, and making homemade art projects, and playing those fun hand-clapping games like Miss Suzie and Down by the Banks, and I know every camp song under the sun. I also have incredible role models: my mother, Polly, Caroline's mother, my amazing grandmas.

I'm thirty-four, and I want what most people want: A partner who loves me for who I am, unconditionally. I want children, and I want so much to be able to look into their eyes and to hear their first words. I want a home full of love and laughter. I hope that this is something that I can, and will, have. I am not going to settle, to feel as though I'm damaged goods because of my disabilities. We all have our shit—mine being, admittedly, big stuff—but I have to believe that the right person is out there for me, someone who wants and needs me as much as I do him. I believe that there is someone, probably several someones, out there for all of us, we just have to open ourselves up: to following our hearts, taking risks, and knowing that nothing is a guarantee, but that true happiness can't come without taking chances.

There are doubts that creep in, though, even as I think about holding a baby in my arms, watching a little kid grow up who inherits my goofy sense of humor or maybe my blue eyes. I know how much a child can learn from having a parent who has a disability, and that it can instill a huge amount of compassion and empathy. I also know, though, that there would be times when he or she would have to make compromises, miss out on things with me, and probably have to learn to do some things on his or her own before other kids. Of course, I would want to teach my children independence and how to handle difficult circumstances, but I would also never, ever want my children to feel the need to take care of me, or be my guide dog, or to ever feel like I couldn't take care of them. To accept help from other people is hard enough.

As sure as I am that I would be a good mother, though, and a joyful one, I believe that if I don't have children, my life will still be rich and full. I have experienced enough uncertainty and loss to know that life is too unpredictable for me to try to guess what's going to happen in the future. Like a lot of single women out there, I'm looking. I have gone on and off of dating sites. I know a singles-guru matchmaker who takes my spin classes who has convinced me to go to many of her events, including a memorable one on a boat, where I spent the evening tottering around in ridiculous heels, the whole thing loud and dark enough that I couldn't see or hear much of anything. As scary as it sometimes is, though, I put myself out there. I'm not closing any doors, but I'm not holding my breath, either.

· · · ·

Finally I got to my door and, as quickly as I could, blurted out, "I'll think about that, Mom. Love you," and hung up the phone before she could get another word in. Maybe I would think about it, but right then I knew Olive was wagging her tail furiously on the other side of the door, desperately waiting to jump all over me as I fumbled to get the key into the lock, never an easy task for me. When I got the door open she leapt into my arms, her licking, panting, joyful puppy love an instant balm, and right then she was all the baby that I needed.

56

As a psychotherapist, a person living with a disability, someone who has recovered from an eating disorder, and someone who has tendencies toward the neurotic and anxious that seem to be as inherited among Jews as the Ashkenazi disorders that we are plagued by, I have spent a fair amount of time thinking about, reading about, and talking about how to live life now.

I need to find the time to take care of myself, emotionally and physically. I have always had energy to spare, and I know I can't calm my brain without working out my body. I need to nurture my relationships, with both friends and family members. I always feel as though I have to take more than my fair share from them, so being there to help and support them in return is hugely important to me. I can't just be the taker. I need to be working toward a goal, to have my sights set on something. The goal can change, but I always need to be focused on something.

Maybe it's just who I am, but, despite all that I have faced, I am happy, and profoundly aware of how fortunate I am. I know that I will do whatever I have to do to protect that happiness and well-being, though it's not always easy. Just like anything else, it takes work, and part of the work is simply feeling satisfied with life and grateful for what I have, and focusing on those things. I think sometimes that because of, not despite, my disabilities and some of the very difficult things that have happened in my life, like my accident, my eating disorder, and Daniel, I am able to make being fulfilled a priority and have found the things that work for me. I believe that people who live very active lifestyles, despite adversity, accept that there is going to be sadness but don't let it take over their lives.

I know that I need to be happy *now*, and, though it's not easy, I can honestly say that I work to create that happiness every day. Of course I'm going to be sad or depressed sometimes, and I'm going to think about how much I'm losing, and have already lost, and need to let myself feel that pain.

After I'm done being sad, though, I'll remember that there are as many wonderful things that I'll get to keep: Olive knocking me over and licking my face in her joyful enthusiasm at seeing me, whether it's been five minutes or five hours; my best friend signing secrets into my palm; the strength of my body; the undying love of my family and friends; my sense of humor; and the ability to help others appreciate what they have.

I try to remember to be in the moment, whatever that is. When I'm taking a bite of food, snuggling with Olive, pedaling as hard as I can on my bike. When someone I love hugs me, I can melt into it and accept it fully for the love that it is.

I appreciate the passing of time. Spring, with its crisp newness, the city feeling cleansed from all the rain. I can smell the sweet, slightly bitter smell of hyacinth wafting from the bodegas and see the flashes of yellow daffodils and purple crocuses as they make their way up from the earth. Fall, with its sense of excitement and longing and nostalgia. Something about the angle of the sun and the way it hits always feels familiar, as though it is tired from the summer and has a softer, lazier feel, not so determined to roast you alive. Metal is no longer hot to the touch, and the loud, irritating hum of air conditioners finally stops. The beginning of fall smells heavier, as the leaves start to bend and color. Time is passing, a year is starting to move toward its close, and I am aware of it, and trying to get all I can from each day.

At the times when my vision is briefly good enough for me to see something that I rarely can, like a star, it feels like a small miracle and can have me smiling for days.

I do think that, for most of us, it's a choice. We can learn to accept the ebb and flow of life, that we wake up in a dynamic body every day, one that is also cyclical and ever changing. Some days, mine can feel different from hour to hour. I'll wake up sometimes thinking, *Hey, I can see pretty well*, and by nighttime I feel as though I can't see a thing. My implant will seem to really improve things one day, and the next I'll be asking, "What?" all day. I have to accept it, because without acceptance I can't live in the present.

57

My disabilities often take turns jockeying for first place in needing attention. For a while my ears were getting most of the attention, as I tried to get used to the implant. As soon as it started to get even the tiniest bit easier, though, I could once again sense that I was experiencing change in my vision.

It seems to be going through another right now. I'm not noticing the hole shrinking much, but what I can see is getting grainy, especially in dim lighting. When I have patients I want to look directly at them for their whole appointment, I owe them that, but it's very exhausting to look in one place, and at one thing, for so long. I can't keep the office as bright as I like, because patients like a quieter, gentler light. I think it can already feel uncomfortable to be spilling out all of your shit to someone; you don't want to feel like you're in an interrogation chamber as well. And, as considerate as they are about whatever I've told them about my disabilities, this is their time, not mine. Most of the time it's good for me to totally focus on someone else and to forget everything else in my life. I have the ability to completely

shut out everything else and concentrate on them. My eyes, however, have more trouble doing that.

Sometimes I now see what look like little white slugs circling
through my line of vision. I can tell that it's something that my
eyes are projecting, like some strange video game floating in front
of me. I hate them. And I hate what they portend. Because what
little vision I have had has been clear. Very limited, but clear. The
clock is ticking louder now.

When I get up in the morning it's not as bad. By the end of
the day, though, my eyes are exhausted, and I want the dark as
much as I want my precious silence.

. . . .

Lately I've been thinking about how I'm really a miracle of modern medicine.

For starters, there's my bionic ear. My wacky, shrill, but nonetheless extraordinary ear. Not to mention my other ear, whose
hearing aids—three of them, all for different environments—
help enormously. I wish I could say that either of these was a perfect fix. They aren't—by a long shot—but they improve my
quality of life immensely.

Then there's my reconstructed foot and all of the shattered
parts in my body that were mended: bones grafted, breaks set,
everything pieced back together like a jigsaw puzzle. Were it not
for the extraordinary doctors who have devoted their lives to research, to whom I owe an enormous debt of gratitude, I would be
almost entirely deaf, mostly blind, and wheelchair-bound.

Then there are my eyes. The big kahuna. I just took my first
vision test in more than two years. I was back in California, and
I met with Dr. Jacque Duncan, a wonderful woman who has

been my primary ophthalmologist for more than fifteen years. Although I had lost more vision, it wasn't any more than what was expected. In fact, when I read the notes that my mother had carefully taken, I saw that in some ways, it had deteriorated less than they thought it would. Still, though, when I got to the end, it read, as it always has, *There is still no treatment or cure for Rebecca's vision loss.*

Even as a skeptic, I can recognize that there might be promise on the horizon. So many people are working toward a cure, using cutting-edge research and methods to try to give me my eyes back, to help so many of us out there. I have to admit that not only am I terrible at science, but I am afraid to get too involved with it all, afraid to spend all of my time hoping, though I am, of course, aware of it. Alan and my parents are wonderful this way; they give me every update, meet with every doctor and researcher, and hunt down every lead. That is something that I would not be able to do myself. Getting through the day is exhausting for me. Although my life is often wonderful and fulfilling, it takes every last drop of energy I have just to get where I need to go, see my patients, teach my classes, spend time with Olive and my friends, and maybe even go on a date. Most of us are probably wiped out after a day in this city that never stops moving, but, since just navigating the sidewalk is a new adventure for me every day, if I didn't give it my all, I couldn't do it. I wouldn't get out of bed. I don't have the time to hunt down the leads and throw myself into the research and still get done all of the things I want to accomplish in my life.

The work that is currently being done on restoring vision is fascinating, though. Stem cell research, gene therapy, and prosthetics have all shown promise, and some people have even gotten limited vision back with them. Dr. Shinya Yamanaka, who won a Nobel Prize in medicine in 2012, is leading one of the first-ever clinical trials using stem cells from a person's own body. MacArthur "Genius Grant" winner Sheila Nirenberg, an extraordinary woman, is working on a gene therapy called optogenetics, which holds great promise for all kinds of retinal diseases. And there are many, many more.

People have encouraged me to get involved in studies before, but doing one can render you unable to do others, and so I'm waiting. Waiting for advancements that will come eventually, soon enough, I hope, to help me, but I refuse to hold my breath. I have to live where I am and to be grateful for the sight that I have. For me there is no other way to live.

58

Last weekend, I went home for my aunt Ellen and aunt Lourdes's wedding. They have been together for thirty-three years and were finally tying the knot now that gay marriage was legal in California. Peter and Alison were there, with beautiful baby Ava. She'd grown so much already, her face had changed, and I longed so much to be able to watch her grow into a little girl, to watch her body lengthen, to see that gorgeous smile on her as a teenager and at her wedding.

Grandma Faye was there, still rocking it at ninety-six, about to embark on her trip to Asia. My father, Polly, Lauren, and Daniel were all there, too. Daniel and I shared a room, and he told me about his plans for the future. He wants to buy a van and live without any help from my parents. At this point, all I want is for my sweet Danny to be happy. I'll always hope for that.

During the reception there was a deejay, and Lauren and I started dancing. Peter got up to join us, with his goofy flair, singing along loudly. Then Alison, who is now like a sister to me, too beautiful to look silly dancing even if she tried. My dad joined in next, doing his usual twist. Daniel got in there, too, still the best dancer, despite everything. The music was so loud that I could really hear it, and it drowned out every other noise. They were familiar, cheesy wedding songs, "Celebration" and "Holiday," songs whose words were forever seared into my brain, so I didn't have to hear them clearly to sing along. I closed my eyes and let myself be fully in the moment, dancing with some of the people I love most in the world. I knew that even when I couldn't see anything anymore, I would be full of joy doing this: dancing, in the dark, surrounded by all the love that I could ever hope for.

I knew, too, that when I flew back to New York, exhausted, Caroline would be there, taking care of Olive, both of them waiting for me to return. I'd ask her to sleep over, and it would be such a relief, after a crazy weekend of family and travel, to finally turn my implant off, take out my hearing aid, and turn out the light. Then we'd lie next to one another, and I'd take her hands and tell her about my weekend, signing my stories into her palms.

Acknowledgments

My list of acknowledgments could span the length of this entire book so please bear with me.

Thank you to the Gotham Books team at Penguin for your teamwork, editing, guidance, and feedback throughout this entire process. Jessica Sindler, Bill Shinker, and Lisa Johnson for your interest and belief in the power of this book. Lauren Marino for taking the reins, editing, and encouraging us to make it the best it could be. Emily Wunderlich, many thanks for your availability and feedback. Thank you to my publicist, Lindsay Gordon, for introducing and promoting this book to everything public and media related and for taking the time to get to know me personally. Thank you, Laura Rossi, for having the same rockin' energy as I do and for helping me overcome my fears of social media—or better yet, handling it for me.

Thank you to my agent, Larry Weissman, who approached me years ago and waited patiently for another five years before approaching me again and convincing me that I had a story people would want to hear.

Acknowledgments

Thank you, Susannah Cahalan, for paving the way with your brave and extraordinary memoir, *Brain on Fire,* and for taking the time to read and improve mine.

Thank you to my extraordinary doctors who have been a part of this journey with me for years. Thank you to Adeline McClatchy, AuD, for being the first to diagnose my hearing loss and thank you, John Diles, AuD, for being my very first audiologist and lifelong friend. If editing would have allowed, I would have included an entire chapter just about you and what an impact you had on my life as a preteen into adulthood. Your office was a safe haven, a place where I felt completely understood. You were an instrumental part of my support team when I needed it most and you have always made me laugh.

Thank you to Dr. Richard Oken and Dr. Marcia Charles-Mo. Marcia, you treated me with so much respect and you listened to me. Thank you for always making me feel very safe and supported in your care.

Dr. Jamie Edmund, you were my very first exposure to therapy. Thank you for your incredible kindness and warmth. I will never forget the time I spent with you. To the Head-Royce School for honoring me so many years later as alumnus of the year. I am still touched by this recognition. Further thanks to Head-Royce for bringing Serena Jones, LCSW, to me. Serena, you have been the most influential clinical social worker in my life to this day.

A tremendous thank-you to Dr. Mark A. Reiley and Dr. Mathias Masem for literally rebuilding the bones of my body and putting me back together again. To my beloved nurse Roberta at Alta Bates and the *many* nurses and hospital staff who cared for me during my extended recovery.

Dr. Jacque Duncan at UCSF Medical Center, your ability to listen and understand vision loss as an emotional experience as

Acknowledgments

well as a clinical one makes me actually *look forward* to seeing you for my otherwise depressing visual exams. Thank you, Dr. Samuel Jacobson at the Scheie Eye Institute, for being one of the leading experts in the very limited research being conducted on Usher syndrome type III. Thank you to the director of otolaryngology at the University of Michigan, Dr. Steven Telian, for your knowledge and expertise and to Dr. Paul Sieving, director of the National Eye Institute and my former ophthalmologist at the University of Michigan. I am still touched by your kindness, communication, and support while I was in your care and trying to come to terms with what was happening to me. To the unstoppable Richard and Cindy Elden, founders of the Usher III Initiative, and the dedicated advisory board members: Dr. David Saperstein, Dr. William Harte, Dr. Samir Patel, and project manager Lindsay Whyte. Here's to believing that a cure is in sight and working vigorously to find it. Thank you to my Usher III sisterhood: Cindy Elden, Wendy Samuelson, Yael Saperstein, and Dana Simon, for your morale and support. Further thanks to Cindy and Wendy for being my support and encouragement when it was my time to go under the knife and be implanted.

To the NYU Langone Cochlear Implant Center and more specifically to world-renowned Dr. J. Thomas Roland and his staff for expertly embedding metal into my skull and carefully inserting all sixteen electrodes into my cochlea. Thank you, Laurel Mahoney, for treating me like an individual despite how many people you see day in and day out and for patiently allowing my entourage to join in on almost every pre- and post-implant appointment. Thank you to speech pathologists Camille Mihalik and Nancy Geller for employing creative techniques while teaching me how to discriminate sounds and learn to hear digitally.

Thank you, Scott Fried, for so fearlessly educating the world about HIV/AIDS from the very beginning. You played a pivotal role in my decision to pursue a career in a helping profession.

Thank you, Nicole Feist and Debbie Fiderer from the Helen Keller National Center, for coordinating and implementing my mobility training.

Thank you, Bill and Tani Austin and the entire team at Starkey Labs Center for Excellence, for all of the years of patience and unending generosity.

To Sonova/Advanced Bionics: Vanessa Erhard Blattman, Kristine Rafter, Katie Skipper, and the rest of the staff for educating and welcoming me into the bionic world and inviting me to share my experience at the Sonova headquarters.

Thank you to Craig Kasper, AuD, for so generously offering your time and professional opinion. To Shelley Borgia, AuD, and the New York Hearing Associates team of professionals, thank you for effectively establishing communication between my hearing aid and my cochlear implant.

To the tireless Maria Bartolillo and Ed McCormack for allowing me to pursue both my personal and professional goals at St. Francis de Sales School for the Deaf. Thank you, Maria, for your ongoing support from afar. You remain an incredible role model to me.

Joni Smith, superheroine, lover of life, and believer in equality, there are no words to describe your strength and character. You encouraged me to learn sign language and embrace my true self. I always hoped that sign language would give me the ability to have language to express to you what you mean to me.

My beloved friends throughout the years who have been with me through all different stages of my vision and hearing loss. Craig Stein, Dave Wesley, and Joe Harrington for being my very first friends with RP and allowing me to know that I am not alone.

From Crocker Highlands, my oldest friends to date, Melissa Neuwelt and Liz Paul, who were my very first best friends and have been with me since the early days.

To the glorious Skylake Yosemite Camp: John T. Howe for giving us "Shasta Call" and soggy "fat pills," Marggi Hamilton Lowenberg, Tyler Fonarow, Jon Moore, Jay Levine, Mark Faughn, Rachel Salzman Adler, Spencer Villasenor, Amos Buhai, Sara Kirsner, Nina Rothberg Bailey, Marni and Amy Merksamer, and the Portnoys for keeping the "Skylake Magic" alive. Special thanks to Rob Yturri for leading by example and showing me how to *live* life with all the love and energy I have in me.

To my beloved Berkeley girls, Hannah Kahn and Meka Kahn Tull, for all of the love and insane laughter you have brought to my life. To this day many of my favorite memories include the two of you. Dan Kemper, you are the most loyal, dedicated, and supportive friend a set of twins could *ever* ask for. Lisa D'Orazio for introducing me to the Santa Barbara crew, Kim Michner Eubank, Sophie Han Akers-Douglas, Monica Isaza, just to name a few. You helped me transition back into life and welcomed me as though I already belonged. More love to Lisa for stepping into my life when I needed a friend most and then never letting go.

From the U of M, Carl Horwitz, Jeremy Miller, Dave Roth, Michelle Ragen Zacchini, and Kristen Korytkowski for being my closest friends and roommates and sharing the best college memories I could have hoped for.

To Harris Cowan, one of my oldest friends in NYC, for helping me move to and from every apartment and being one of my fiercest supporters. Thank you, Michelle Ho, for being a wonderful friend and for your ability to listen without passing judgment.

To the unbelievable team at The Fhitting Room in NYC for

helping me maintain my sanity on a daily basis with your infectious energy and passion for what you do.

Thank you, Keith Gornish and Sean Rogers, for introducing me to functional fitness and for teaming up with me to "crush" every Civilian Military Combine (CMC) I am a part of.

Thank you to Monique Dash, Cathe Thompson, Rachel Sibony, and the rest of the Equinox team for all of the years of support and encouragement you have given me to be the best fitness instructor I can be. Thank you, Lisa Gausepohl from the Sports Club LA, for never giving up on me despite my challenges. And thank you, Maryann Donner from New York Health and Racquet, for genuinely caring about the well-being of your instructors.

Thank you to the entire Baker family for filling my childhood with so many wonderful shared family memories.

To my family. My twin brother and my other half, my pride and joy, the one person I can sit with in person or on the phone for hours without even saying a word and feel both at peace and at home. Your open mind, patience, and awareness of yourself and others are only a glimpse into what makes you a true lover of life and so brilliant. Peter, we share the same heart and soul and love of humanity. You have the incredible ability to make me cry with laughter. Alison, I was beside myself the day I learned I would finally have a little sister. I never could have anticipated that I would later gain a big sister as well. I am forever touched by the way in which you and your family have embraced me. Precious Ava, I can't wait to see your hands form their first signs. Lauren, you were born into a complicated family and remain the toughest and most strong-minded of us all. Dad, for passing on your undeniable sense of humor, your belief in community, helping others, and fighting for justice. Your children have always been your livelihood. Pol, this book does not come close to describing the force you have been and continue to be in my life. You are the glue to our family and the reason we are all even partially sane. Mom, you have always incorporated your creativity into the way you express love for your children, stepchildren, family, and friends. You are loyal, honest, and incredibly thoughtful. You taught me the importance of listening in order to understand. John, you have been a rock throughout this wild ride that is the Alexander family. Mikey, you taught me the crucial importance of boundaries, and Pete and Sarah, I admire you for your open minds and your patience. Aunt Ellen and Aunt Lourdes for being my prime example of what it means to be in love after all of these years. To Susanne and Larry Kaczor for including me as a part of your family and loving me as though I am one of your own.

To my marvelous grandmothers: Grandma Etta for always being exactly who you are and never pretending to be anyone that you're not. Your ability to listen and share your wisdom have helped me greatly. Grandma Faye, you moved across the country to be present in our lives as we grew up, and for that you have been my confidante, my caretaker, and my best friend. Thank you for always reminding me that "nobody promised me a rose garden." The strength of you both is carried further out into the world through me.

Olive, my sweet baby girl, the biggest pain in my ass, and the best snuggler *ever*. You are living proof that the love you give is the love you get back. Alan, you know and understand me better than anyone else in the world. I have learned from you since the day we met, and I continue to learn from you to this day. You are the most intelligent, loyal, respectful, insightful, optimistic, and hysterical person I know. There are no words to truly describe what you mean to me. Caroline, you are my teammate. Your willingness to take my hand and face our fears as best friends has been remarkable. You have taught me the power of communication and learning how to practice commitment.

Sascha, thank you for listening to me and for always asking questions. Thank you for dedicating so much time and energy to bringing my story to life. And thank you for always keeping my stomach full with so much delicious food!